Washington State Football 1915

Back Row

William "Lonestar" Dietz, Silas Stites, Ray Loomis, Clarence Zimmerman, Ray Finney, Asst. Coach Tommy Tyrer, Athletic Director "Doc" Bohler

Middle Row

Arthur Durham, Ralph Boone, Ronald Fishback, Carl Dietz, Carl King, Capt. Asa "Ace" Clark, Walter Herreid, Benton Bangs

Front Row

Alfred Langdon, Basil Doane, Harry Applequist, Frank Michaels, Dick Hanley, Clarence Boone, Bert Brooks

CHANCE
FOR GLORY

THE INNOVATION AND TRIUMPH OF THE 1916
WASHINGTON STATE ROSE BOWL TEAM

DARIN WATKINS

AVIVA
PUBLISHING
New York

CHANCE FOR GLORY
The Innovation and Triumph of the Washington State 1916 Rose Bowl Team

Copyright @2015 Darin Watkins

Published by:
Aviva Publishing
Lake Placid, NY
(518) 523-1320
www.AvivaPubs.com

Address all inquiries to:
Darin Watkins
Address: 1410 NW State St, Pullman WA 99163
Phone: (509) 332-8523
Email: info@chance4glory.com
Website: chance4glory.com

ISBN: 978-1-943164-48-6

Library of Congress: 2015915609

Editor: Tyler Tichelaar
Cover Design: Nicole Gabriel, Angel Dog Productions
Interior Book Design: Nicole Gabriel, Angel Dog Productions

Every attempt has been made to source properly all quotes.

Printed in the United States of America

First Edition

CONTENTS

Cast of Characters   7

Preface   11

Chapter 1:   Beginnings   13

Chapter 2:   Oregon   77

Chapter 3:   Oregon Agricultural College   97

Chapter 4:   Idaho   123

Chapter 5:   Montana   141

Chapter 6:   Whitman   159

Chapter 7:   Gonzaga   173

Chapter 8:   Rose Bowl   195

Chapter 9:   Endings   237

Bibliography   249

CAST OF CHARACTERS

GLENN "POP" WARNER
Football coach – Carlisle Indian School

ENOCH BRYAN
President of Washington State College

WILLIAM "LONESTAR" DIETZ
Football Coach – Washington State
College

ARTHUR "BULL" DURHAM
Quarterback

BENTON BANGS
Running Back

ASA "ACE" CLARK
Football Team Captain

"DOC" BOHLER
Trainer, Assistant Coach, and Athletic Director

CLARENCE ZIMMERMAN
Offensive and Defensive Lineman

DICK HANLEY
Wide Receiver

ALFRED LANGDON
Center

RONALD FISHBACK
Linebacker

HACK APPLEQUIST
Offensive Lineman

CARL DIETZ
Full Back

PREFACE

Once upon a time, outside a Cougar football game, a man named Girard Clark told me the most amazing story. It was about the 1915 Washington State football team, an adventurous tale of undersized players who through a combination of innovative strategies and sheer will marched their way to the first championship Rose Bowl game. His father, Asa Clark, had been the captain.

In the two decades since, I have diligently looked up newspaper clippings and accounts of games, spent hours in WSU's manuscript and archive collection, and listened to stories from families and fans to uncover and separate the facts from the folklore. After all, this is a story based on handed-down tales and written words of events that happened one hundred years ago.

It begins with the coach, William "Lone Star" Dietz, who remains a revered figure at WSU. He led its teams to the greatest football accomplishments ever recorded, and he did it during a time when racial parity was a long way off. He made the lives of those he touched better and gave the men under him the gift of imagination—the ability to see themselves in a light brighter than any of them believed possible. He believed the only label that counts is the one you put on yourself.

But this is a story that is about more than football. It's about a young college striving for recognition and survival in a state dominated by its older brother, the University of Washington. Success for this team ran parallel to the school's victories with state lawmakers.

My deepest thanks to Mark O'English, John Paxson, Scott and James Brewer, Thomas White, Karla Schubach, Bill Gardner, Tyler Tichelaar, Patrick Snow, Kari Montgomery, and Ruth, Garrick, and Delaney Watkins for helping me craft this wonderful book.

I love this story. It's a great WSU treasure long-forgotten.

To the WSC football team of 1915—welcome back.

Go Cougs!
Darin Watkins

CHAPTER 1

BEGINNINGS

THE GAME

West Point, New York
November 9, 1912

The game of college football was ruled by the mighty and the powerful.

Standing among the best was the U.S. Military Academy at West Point, a team that relied on brute force to bully its way through the competition. The Cadets had a storied tradition of playing so aggressively that it was not uncommon for opponents to land in the hospital. The academy itself was built around the simple premise of training leaders for war. Their services were greatly needed. Earlier in the year, the U.S. had invaded both Nicaragua and Cuba. The first Balkan War had broken out with Bulgaria, Serbia, and Greece fighting Turkey—the very conflict that would draw in neighboring countries, eventually leading the rest of the world into war.

But on this blustery day in November, thoughts of armed conflict were set aside for a heavily-anticipated game of football—a contest between two of the season's best. This one would be settled under gray skies before a crowd of over 5,000 fans in the stadium nestled near the Hudson River, where cool temperatures triggered a heavy gray mist that drifted onto the field.

West Point vs. Carlisle

The West Point Cadets, with only one loss on the 1912 season, were the team to beat. They were led by Capt. Leland Devore, a behemoth of a man, 6'6" with 250 pounds of sheer muscle. Standing next to him was a bruiser named Alexander Weyland, a heavyweight with a pounding style. Lined up, shoulder-to-shoulder, the pair formed the point of a wedge that simply drove their opponents back. Much was made of their style of play the year before when two Yale players were hospitalized and nearly killed trying to stand directly in their way. In the backfield was running back and future Army general, Dwight Eisenhower, who spoke of how he "loved the feel of slamming into an opponent." At only 5'8", this blonde-haired, blue-eyed character may have stood shorter than his larger teammates, but he carried with him a fierce determination. As a two-way player, he would lead the running game on offense, while racking up the most tackles on the team as a linebacker on defense. For Eisenhower, the way he played spoke volumes about his character; he told a reporter, "I so loved the bodily contact of football that I suppose my enthusiasm made up somewhat for my lack of size."

The West Point team stood at the pinnacle of American football, a human monument to power and strength.

Facing them on this heavily anticipated day would be the Carlisle Indian School from Pennsylvania, a dynamic team with one of the best records in the nation on the season at 10-0-1. The college included Native Americans from 140 tribes from across the country. Using speed and an unorthodox style, the team had risen through the ranks by deploying new formations and uncanny deceptive style in the backfield. At the core of the Carlisle charge stood Jim

Thorpe, arguably one of the greatest athletes of his day, having just won two Olympic Gold Medals in the decathlon and pentathlon. He wasn't alone. Quarterback Gus Welch was blessed with a slight-of-hand that brilliantly confused defenders. In a signature style, Welch would call out a play by muttering just a few words, or by using hand gestures and snapping the ball before the defense had a chance to get set.

Despite the racial tensions of the era, this Carlisle team carried a true swagger on the field, often taunting opposing players and making funny remarks as the game progressed. After one play where the referee gave Carlisle a bad spot with the ball, one player remarked, "What's the use of crying about a few inches when the white man has taken the whole country?" In another contest, with their opponent's defense left exhausted from the constant speedy barrage, the quarterback Welch taunted defenders by declaring, "We're going to run the ball to the right." They did, and despite the warning of their intentions, gained 20 yards. Carlisle's style of play led the nation in scoring, marching its way past East Coast dynasties such as Syracuse, Georgetown, and Pittsburgh.

For years, the U.S. government had opposed a matchup between these two teams. Only a generation before, General Custer had been defeated in the Battle of Little Bighorn. It had been a little over two decades since the U.S. Army had attacked the Lakota tribe at Wounded Knee. Feelings were still raw. Only a few weeks earlier, *The New York Times* had reported, "When Indian outbreaks in the West were frequent the Government officials thought it unwise to have the aborigines and future officers combat in athletics, but this state has passed." The game would be allowed. Make no mistake; this game was for far more than national bragging rights. This game would be a clash of football theologies and the first real challenge to the traditional style of power football. All from an upstart team with a dynamic new approach.

Leading the way on the Carlisle sideline stood Coach "Pop" Warner, a grumpy curmudgeon of a man who often paced up and down the sidelines, with a hand-rolled lit cigarette dangling from his mouth. The forty-two-year-old coach, with his dark curly hair and barrel chest, had long waited for this game. Despite his disheveled appearance, Warner was at heart a brilliant tactician. On this day, he had a few surprises in store for the Army team.

It had been Warner himself who had once dismissed Jim Thorpe for not being adequate enough to play football. When Thorpe first showed up at Carlisle, he was just another gangly kid in overalls. One day, walking casually across the athletic field, Thorpe ran up to the school's high-jump bar and cleared it with ease. Other track athletes could only stand by in awe. Thorpe had just cleared 5'3", a height that would have been a school record. When word of the jump reached Warner, the coach reached out to Thorpe to turn out for track. The eighteen-year-old Thorpe had recently lost his father, so with the promise of playing sports and the fatherly approach of Warner, Thorpe would be convinced to stay at Carlisle to finish his education.

As the Carlisle track coach, Warner knew Thorpe could be something special, and he trained him all the way through to the Olympics. But it was on the football field where Thorpe could really shine. An athletic specimen with amazing speed who could do it all—dodge opponents with a crafty ability to switch direction, or power his way through, carrying players 10 yards down the field— Thorpe could also pull up and throw the ball 60 yards, or kick it just as far. But in the beginning, Warner did not want the boy to play football. "I'm sorry, son, but you're just not big enough," he once told the young Thorpe. Pointing to players getting ready to practice, Thorpe gestured for Warner to give him the ball, saying, "Oh, c'mon coach; you have to give me a chance." Reluctantly, Warner agreed. The drill involved trying to weave through some three dozen players on the field. Thorpe took off like a jackrabbit, running left, then stopping short, and quickly shooting off in the other direction. Running virtually untouched, Thorpe continued on until most of the players gave up out of exhaustion. Rambling back up the sidelines, he tossed Warner the ball, saying, "I gave them some good practice, didn't I, Pop?" Warner just stood there amazed. He had no choice but to let Thorpe on the team.

Warner himself had traveled to tribes all across the country, convincing mothers and fathers to let him bring their sons to Carlisle. Young Native Americans—some of them from the poorest edges of the country—were now forged together as a team. Their differences had become their strength. Their victories had given them character.

But to Coach Warner on this day in November, something was not quite right with his usually brash team. Walking into the locker room, he found his twenty-two men huddled together, quiet and sullen. Only Jim Thorpe was standing, and nervously pacing around the wooden benches. The players had long since laced up their ankle-high, leather, cleated shoes with thick soles, while their baggy wool pants with the smell of the long football season clung close to their skin. On the front of their sweaters was a large C, and flannel was stuffed around their shoulders for padding. Leather helmets sat waiting with flap-ears, each well-worn into the shape of each player's head after a season of play. Time was running out just before kick-off. Warner wasn't one for big speeches, but looking into his players' eyes, he knew they needed something that would help them stand for themselves—something to set aside the fear of playing against the U.S. Army.

Stepping before them with a fierce look of determination, Warner spoke, "On every play, I want all of you to remember one thing: your fathers and your grandfathers are the ones who fought their fathers. These men playing against you today are soldiers. They are the Long Knives. You are Indians. Tonight, we will know if you are warriors. Let's go!" With that, the players leaped up in unison, heading outside with new determination.

As Warner glanced around the stadium, he must have been struck by a seemingly colorless landscape as the teams warmed up on the field. The football stands were almost uniformly gray, the color of the wool tunics of the West Point cadets on hand to cheer their team. Intense anticipation came from the cadet side of the field as well. Eisenhower himself had long awaited this contest, believing he would be the one to knock Thorpe from the game. Having won the toss, Carlisle would receive. The crowd roared as the high kick landed into the hands of Jim Thorpe on the 15-yard line. Racing up the middle, he would be brought down on the 30-yard line.

Warner had sent scouts ahead to watch the Cadets play, so he knew their favorite tactic was to push straight up the middle on defense. He had to smile. His team had been working on a new formation for weeks, for just this moment. As Warner's Carlisle boys lined up, quarterback Gus Welch called out the first audible, causing the backs to split out to both sides. It would be football's first double-wing formation, one that Warner had devised just for this contest. His plan was to neutralize Army's strength by buttoning it up from the outside. The wings, near the line of scrimmage, would effectively seal in the outside tackles. This formation also multiplied the number of options available to the team for sweeps, reverses, or any number of pitches or passes.

On the very first play, Carlisle quarterback Gus Welch pitched the ball out to his halfback Alex Arcasa, who sprinted from right to left for 15 yards behind the blocking of Thorpe. No sooner was he down than the team sprinted back into formation without pausing to huddle. With the same formation, another wide pitch was open to Arcasa, running to the right. Suddenly, the back stopped, looked left, and threw the ball to the other side of the field to Thorpe for a 15-yard pass. Just like that, Carlisle had moved the ball into Army territory for a first down, a feat few teams had accomplished that season. Pop Warner smiled to himself. "The shifting, puzzling and dazzling attack of the Carlisle Indians had the Cadets bordering on a panic," *The New York Tribune* would report.

Three plays later, Carlisle used the same play. As Army chased Arcasa to the right, he pulled up and passed again to Thorpe, who was out in the open field. This time, Army linebacker Dwight Eisenhower was ready. Taking a bead on the speedy runner, Eisenhower saw his chance and put a huge hit on Thorpe. He wasn't alone. From the other side, a second Army player reached Thorpe at the exact same moment. The massive collision could be heard from the stands. Thorpe was stunned and lost the ball. Army would recover deep in its own territory.

As the play cleared, Warner's heart sank. There lay Jim Thorpe, rolling on the ground in pain, holding his right shoulder. The Army tradition of trying to knock a man out of the game appeared to have worked. Warner and others raced to Thorpe's side. The first thing the coach did was to feel along Thorpe's shoulder blade to see whether there were any breaks—there weren't. The referee pointed to his watch and said, "Coach, we'll need to move him on a stretcher."

"Hell's bells, Mr. Referee," said Lenore, the Army Captain, "let's give him all the time he needs."

It was in that singular moment that everything changed.

Thorpe jumped to his feet as if nothing had happened and ran to the sideline, lightly rubbing his shoulder. The attempt by the Army captain to be gracious appeared to have struck Thorpe as condescending. From that point on, Thorpe played with a heightened sense of determination. Angered by what had happened, Carlisle fullback Stancil "Possum" Powell punched the Army quarterback Vern Pritchard. Powell was ejected from the game, and the penalty gave Army the ball at the Indians' 25-yard line.

The Cadets lined up for their power style of play. Briefly, it seemed Carlisle's defense might hold. The defenders rarely stayed still before the snap, which gave the Army offense trouble in figuring out just whom they were supposed to block. But Army answered by switching to a tight, sweeping formation. A powerful flow of men and movement followed by the running back Dwight Eisenhower eagerly flattened any defender along the way. In just a few plays, Army had its first down on the Carlisle 15-yard line. Almost with ease, Eisenhower again took the ball and followed his blockers around the right side untouched, marching deftly into the end zone. Army took an early 6-0 lead, a botched extra point attempt and the only mark against a flawless drive. The sound of cannon rocked the stadium from the south end zone. Fans celebrated in the stands, believing the game was well in hand. With little emotion, the Army players simply dusted themselves off and lined up to kick.

Unlike most teams of the day, Carlisle used completely different players for offense and defense, giving Warner a freshly rested team for each change of possession. On offense, the full force of Warner's coaching chicanery came into view. Sweeps suddenly turned into reverses. Grand gestures to take the ball into the line left defenders rushing forward to make a tackle on players who suddenly didn't have the ball. A simple pitch by quarterback Welch to Arcasa sprinting to the right became a reverse to a sprinting Thorpe going left. When Army seemed to have the runner corralled in the backfield, Carlisle would suddenly stop and throw the ball deep downfield. Play after play, the offense appeared to be performing a well-rehearsed ballet. Soon, Carlisle found itself on the Army 8-yard line. The drive would end as strangely as it had begun: a trick play where the center snapped the ball, dropped back to block, then while the backs took off in both directions, Quarterback Gus Welch faked left, then right, then quietly handed the ball to his blocking center, who charged up the middle for an easy score. With the extra point, it was now Carlisle in the lead 7-6. Fans grew silent at this sudden change.

When the Carlisle defense returned to the field, its players resumed their constantly moving style of play, using their speed and agility to maneuver around the power blocking attack. Defenders stepped away from powerful blocks only to nip at the running backs from the side. Army could still move the ball, but it could only manage a few yards at a time. Suddenly, Army found itself failing to make a first down. Carlisle would take a one-point lead into halftime.

In the locker room, the Army players were frustrated with their performance. Eisenhower pulled aside his fellow linebackers to make plans to "take out" Thorpe. Fans often referred to it as "the ol' one-two," with one player striking up high in the chest, the other taking out the legs. It was a devious plan that had been used effectively this season, and it would now be used against Carlisle's most powerful weapon.

Thorpe seemed stronger in the second half than in the first. On the team's first possession, Thorpe sprinted from side to side, knocking defenders to the ground with a devastating stiff arm. When it seemed Army had Thorpe cornered, he would suddenly pull up and throw the ball deep with surprising accuracy. When he didn't have the ball, he proved to be a devastating blocker. With his team lined up near the end zone, Thorpe and Joe Guyon doubled up on Army's leading tackler, Leland Devore, with a surprisingly powerful blow. Right behind them, the Carlisle running back Arcasa all but strolled into the end zone, giving his team a 14-6 lead.

The block left Devore enraged. On the ensuing kick-off, Devore appeared to take his frustrations out by running full speed into Carlisle's Guyon, who never saw the blow coming. Devore's hit drove the smaller player to the ground and left him unconsciousness. Pandemonium threatened to take over the game as emotions now ran high. After a brief huddle, the referees ejected Devore for "unsportsmanlike conduct." Eisenhower knew that without his best blocker and best defender, the game would be on his shoulders. His plan to take out Thorpe seemed even more critical to the outcome. After three plays, Army was forced to punt. With Carlisle back on offense, Ike would have his chance.

Nearly everyone in the stands knew that on first down, Thorpe would be getting the ball. On the snap, Welch spun around to buy

Thorpe a moment for the blockers to do their work. The Carlisle offense continued to weave in a series of confusing misdirection movements, timed to open up a hole in the middle of the Army line that Thorpe raced through at full speed. This was the moment Eisenhower and Hobbs had waited for. The two linebackers lowered their heads with a full burst of energy, smashing into Thorpe from two sides. Eisenhower would later say it was among the hardest hits he had ever delivered. The collision could be heard from the top of the stands.

As the whistle sounded, players moved back to reveal all three men lying face down on the ground. Thorpe appeared to have taken the brunt of the punishment. For the moment, it appeared Eisenhower and Hobbs had won; they had just taken down the greatest athlete of their time. But that moment of victory quickly vanished as Thorpe jumped to his feet and ran back behind the line as if nothing had happened. Gus Welch was among the first to stop him. "You O.K.?" he asked. Thorpe, nodding his head, appeared to be completely unfazed, even eager to keep moving forward. The other two men were slow to get up.

A few plays later, Thorpe sprinted straight into the heart of the Army defense once again. Head down, he knew the punishment headed his way. Eisenhower eagerly raced forward to finish the job. This time, it would be Ike's teammate Charles Benedict who flew into the melee. All three barreled straight toward each other in a repeat of the exact same collision. Eisenhower couldn't believe he was getting a second chance. With even more determination than before, he propelled himself toward the sprinting Thorpe.

Yet at the very instant the trio would collide, something changed. Thorpe went from a full-speed run into an immediate stop. The

Army linebackers, already committed to a violent collision, slammed directly into each other with a tremendous force. Thorpe, with an almost comical gesture, stopped, and then cut around the pair for another substantial gain. Tossing the ball back to the referee, he glanced back to see the two Army linebackers writhing on the ground, dazed and nearly unconscious. As Eisenhower regained his sense, he tried to stand only to feel a shooting pain ripping through his right knee. Benedict stumbled over to the sidelines. Eisenhower tried to stay in the game, but on the very next play, he would be removed by the Army coach.

With the power trio from Army off the field, Thorpe played the game of his life—at one point twisting into the air to snag a pass from Welch that was well over his head. Another touchdown gave Carlisle a 21-6 lead. Eisenhower, with his leg wrapped in an ice bag, could watch no more, and carrying his helmet, he wandered away from the field of play. When it was all over, Carlisle would win the game 28-6. Sportswriters swarmed all around Thorpe, who had just run for over 200 yards against one of the nation's best teams. He was now raised to elite status among the most popular football athletes of his day. As for Dwight Eisenhower, the disappointment was crushing. His roommate and closest friend would write that he had "lost interest in life," and was content merely to exist until graduation set him free.

On the train ride home from the game, Pop Warner couldn't stop himself from smiling. He had achieved more than he had ever imagined possible. His tactics had paid off. His validation was right there on the train in front of him. As the train moved along, the team gathered around a white-haired man who had shown a keen interest in their performance. His name was Walter Camp, the former Yale quarterback, a former coach and advanced tactician in his own right, whom many hailed as "The Father of Football." His words carried enormous weight in newspaper columns and football forums. Every year, his own personal selection for All-American football players was printed in newspapers across the land. And here he sat, listening intently to every word, occasionally offering up his own thoughts and insights. "Your quarterback calls the plays too fast," Camp offered. "He doesn't study the defense." To which Jim Thorpe himself answered: "How can he study the defense when there isn't any." Camp listened, and then he spoke openly of how the game might be forever changed. He was intrigued by the possibilities of the wing formation used by Carlisle.

As the train carried the men back to their school and student life, no one realized that Camp's account of the game would be picked up by newspapers and publications nationwide. His words would inspire a new way of thinking about the game. This game had proven that speed and strategy could overcome power and strength. In truth, this victory would change college football, inspiring coaches and leaders alike.

From this single game would be born a dream—a dream that would profoundly change the lives of those living 2,500 miles away in the eastern Washington town of Pullman.

Home to Washington State College.

DUPLICITY

Pullman, Washington
March 1915

A dangerous storm ahead threatened the survival of Washington State College, and its president, Enoch Bryan, had grown weary of the constant struggle. Standing in his office, he peered out the window, his reflection an aged reminder of his time in this place. For twenty-two years, he had fought desperately to carve out an institution of higher learning in the hills of the Palouse. A simple name, yet a concept so powerful—this was Washington State College.

But all he had achieved was now at risk.

It was a dream first articulated by Abraham Lincoln and others who willed the country to bring education to the people. "That all men and women of this great land might be educated." Enoch Bryan lived by those words and took pride in his work to modernize and improve until not a single brick remained from the earliest days of the college. And while visitors saw new buildings, he saw dreams rising—a testament to the idea of a land-grant college

Yet this feeling of a job well-done quickly faded with a glance down at the letter in his hand. It was written by lawmakers from the other side of the state. No single word conjured up more frustration for Bryan than "duplicity." A legislative commission had been formed to examine whether the teaching of several lines of education at Washington State College "duplicated" those offered by the University of Washington.

It was a fight that may have been inevitable.

How Bryan had tired of the ugly labels given to his college by supporters of the University of Washington, based in Seattle. Derogatory phrases such as "cow college" and "hayseed students" were used by those who demeaned his own efforts to build support for their "bigger brother" to the west. The letter in his hand now confirmed his greatest fears. Two experts were being brought to the college by the investigating commission. Both were bluebloods, through and through—a Harvard professor of education, and a transplanted New Englander who had years of study in Europe. Neither had any concept of the land-grant movement, its history, or its mission. As the legislature wrapped up its work for 1915, it revealed that for the next year, this "duplicity" committee was charged with developing a final report to the governor himself, outlining each school's responsibilities, as well as establishing a funding commitment needed from taxpayers.

Bryan saw that Washington State College was headed for a fight for its very survival.

Only a month earlier, the University of Washington had hired a young leader. Shy of his fortieth birthday, Henry Suzzallo had been appointed by the Board of Regents as president. The brash professor of philosophy had once been superintendent of schools in San Francisco, but he brought an Ivy League style to his educational leadership. Publically, Suzzallo spoke of the need to "restrict Washington State College to strictly agricultural pursuits—tear down those buildings now committed to science—and turn over some 100,000 acres of land, endowed by the federal government, to the University of Washington for scientific advancement."

Suzzallo's challenge was not new. It had just been elevated to a new threat.

Bryan could only shake his head at the enormity of it all. Despite his letters to the state's leading editors, it seemed newspapers gave more attention to his college's football problems than it did to the legislative winds of change. The previous football season had ended in disaster. The WSC eleven finished off a 2-4 season with a humiliating loss to the University of Washington 45-0. His head coach John Bender had originally been a popular choice by a faculty committee having played for WSC. But the Board of Regents had spoken. Bender would not be back. Bryan knew he needed to find a coach on his own and within the month.

Part of being a visionary leader is allowing oneself to imagine greatness. Bryan often contemplated the story of an undersized team from Carlisle defeating its own nemesis, the mighty West Point Army cadets. East Coast football had become a national sensation. Twenty-thousand fans often lined up to see college games. More important than numbers, the game brought together people from all walks of life under a single banner of pride.

But Washington State's own nemesis, the University of Washington, had become so dominant it now said it would never play Washington State again. After all, the "U" had beaten his boys and had beaten them badly for nearly a decade. To make matters worse, the college teams of the Northwest were joining those from California to form a Pacific Coast Conference. This season might be WSC's last chance to assert its own claim for membership. But Bryan had an idea of where to turn if he wanted to try something bold—he recalled a game played out a few years earlier in New York, where a small college had defeated one of the nation's most powerful football dynasties.

Calling in his assistant, Bryan knew time was of the essence. A telegram would be sent to Coach Glenn "Pop" Warner at the Carlisle Indian School. It was a long shot, but Bryan asked but one simple question: Was there someone Warner might recommend for the Washington State job? Privately, many believed President Bryan wanted to hire Jim Thorpe.

In truth, Bryan was tired of playing defense.

GLENN "POP" WARNER

Carlisle Indian School
March 1915

For Glenn "Pop" Warner, the Carlisle Indian School's rise to fame would be in part responsible for its downfall. As the miracle football season of 1912 came to a close, fans from all across the region would flock to see the team practice. Among those fans one fateful day was Charles Glancy, a baseball coach who spent his summers working as a minor-league baseball manager. The Carlisle school had come to Worcester, Massachusetts, for its last game of the season against Brown University. Like many, Glancy wanted to get a look at Jim Thorpe.

Glancy was *stunned* by what he saw.

This football player was the same *James Thorpe* who had played semi-professional baseball so magnificently for him in the East Carolina league. Excited, Glancy leaned over to a young sports reporter from the local paper named Roy Johnson.

"You should see him play baseball," said Glancy.

"See who play baseball?" asked a distracted Johnson.

Glancy went on to tell the reporter how Thorpe had played semi-professional baseball on the Rocky Mount Railroaders back in 1909 and 1910. Johnson was skeptical. But in the days that followed, a check of the Carolina league roster revealed the truth. Jim Thorpe's name was listed on the roster of the professional team. While it wasn't uncommon for college players to play semi-pro ball, most would use an alias. Thorpe, apparently not understanding the risk it posed to his amateur status, had not.

It would be a revelation that would stun the sporting world. It meant that by definition, Thorpe had been a professional athlete when he competed in the Olympics. The implications would soon be known. When confronted, Thorpe had admitted to doing both. He didn't believe there was a problem. But the discovery would have a profound impact on Thorpe and the people around him. Within months, Thorpe would be stripped of his Olympic medals and his beloved Carlisle school would be cast into controversy. Warner and others would be called to Congressional hearings with new charges the team had provided athletes with clothes, food, and even spending money while at the school. Carlisle and its leaders were cleared, but the damage had been done. Athletics would now become a minor part of the educational process at the school.

With all that he had built in jeopardy, Pop Warner chose to accept the head coaching position at the University at Pittsburgh. Glancing at the array of photos on the wall, memories began to rush past—the trick play he used against Pennsylvania, the new scheme he used against Army. Yes, some of his methods were a bit "unorthodox," but they were good enough to land him a coveted position at a new college. The journey had been a long one for Warner. It first began while he attended law school at Cornell. While most saw football as a contest of force, Warner saw it as a moving game of chess—a battle of the mind as much as a physical battle on the field.

In the midst of change, a telegram arrived. It was from the President of Washington State College; he was looking for a new football coach. As Warner considered the options, one man's name came immediately to mind: his assistant coach, William "Lone Star"

Dietz. Like many at the school, Dietz had taken on a traditional name while retaining his given Indian name. Originally from the Lakota Sioux tribes, Dietz had played on the early powerhouse teams with Thorpe and had proven to be one of his most trusted assistants.

But William Dietz was a hard man to figure out. Dietz was an artist and an instructor, often labeled as being a "dandy" for his constant attention to fashion. Life had not been easy for the young Dietz, with his mother a Sioux Indian and his father a German-born engineer. He had recently married a professor, an established Indian artist several years his senior. But Dietz also had a passion for the game of football. His game management rivaled any. His strategies cut along the same lines as Warner in their innovations and ability to modify schemes to fit the skill levels of his players, who included athletes overmatched by their opponents.

Dietz too had options. There had been speculation Dietz would take over the Carlisle program. Warner had even given some thought to taking Dietz with him to Pittsburgh.

No, Dietz seemed destined for something bigger. After thinking the matter over, Warner came to a decision. He would give his strongest recommendation for the Washington State College job to William Dietz. After all, football on the West Coast had begun to gain strong interest, and the timing might be right for someone with a new vision.

That someone would be William "Lone Star" Dietz.

Search

Joseph Ashlock loved working as the personal assistant to Washington State President Enoch Bryan. But this task at hand made the job very uncomfortable. What President Bryan had asked of him was to lead the search for a new football coach—and to conclude negotiations all within one month. There would be no faculty search. No sports committee recommendation. No real time to search out all the potential candidates. The mood on campus wasn't good. Behind the scenes was plenty of internal strife when it came to talking about the football program.

In his hand, Ashlock held the application of Dietz, along with ten others from men who had written or sent telegrams about the job. This would be no easy task. President Bryan made it clear the work was to be done quietly and quickly. For several weeks, Ashlock had sent out inquiries and asked leaders for references. E.R. Wingard from Maine emerged as one of the top contenders. Yet a U.S. Congressman soon became involved in recommending Dietz. Ashlock had gathered all the information he could on such short notice.

It was time for him to report his findings directly to the president.

University of Washington Football

Across the state, the University of Washington football program geared up for yet another grand season. At the helm was Gilmour "Gloomy Gil" Dobie, a stern taskmaster of a man who ran his football program like a well-oiled military machine. The newspapers liked to color him with words like "crusty" or "grumpy." But the words only served to help add some humanity to Dobie's dour character. Yet few could challenge his unbelievable record. In his seven seasons at the "U," his men had never once been defeated, amassing a record of 45-0 with two ties.

During the last meeting between the University of Washington and Washington State College, Dobie's team had been nothing short of dominating, winning the contest 45-0. But the score really didn't do the game justice. Dobie's team had kept State pinned down into its end of the field for the entire game.

The political atmosphere within his university was to play down the role of the "other" college in the state, which Dobie had used to his advantage. He hated traveling to Pullman, and after this last game, he made the bold declaration that Washington State was of such a poor quality he would vow never to set foot in Pullman again to play "such an undeserving team." Therefore, Dobie watched with interest to see who might take the job. John Bender had been a decent enough coach, but he was told he would not be retained. It didn't turn out so bad for Bender, who despite a dismal football record the previous season of only 2-4, had convinced the leadership at Kansas State to hire him as their new football coach.

Dobie wondered whom State might get, but he wasn't too worried. After all, he had successfully dropped Washington State off the schedule for any future games.

Decisions

President Bryan was running out of options. He had promised the Board of Regents a new coach would be in place within one month. What he needed to offer his fan base was hope—something that would add excitement and build support for his school. On his desk were the names of the various candidates available for the job. Many high school coaches were enthusiastic to make the jump to the college level, while several coaches from smaller colleges were more than eager to take the position. Bryan knew a decision had to be made, and made quickly.

The most intriguing option would be William Dietz. Although untested, Dietz came with the highest praise from Pop Warner. It wasn't lost on Bryan that this man was also half Native American. Bryan remained captivated by the stories he had read of the Carlisle football team that had toppled giants. As he stared out the window, pondering his options, he asked the waiting Ashlock a simple question: "How do you feel about us hiring a Native American to lead our team?"

Ashlock finally had his chance to express his apprehensions. "Well, I don't believe it would be well-received," he answered. "There are plenty of those with influence in our community who would say, "The only good Indian is a dead Indian." As soon as the words left his mouth, Ashlock knew he was in trouble. He would remember those words for years to come, even admitting to them in personal letters to future leaders.

Bryan's face began to betray a quiet anger, an emotion this college leader rarely displayed. Without speaking, the president turned back to the window, quietly searching for answers. Final decisions must always fall on the shoulders of leaders.

Bryan set aside his trepidation and stepped boldly into the unknown. He would tell Ashlock to offer the position to Dietz. To ensure the college could compete with other schools to get his new coach, a contract was drawn up to pay Dietz a salary of $2,250— roughly what the top professors of the day were paid.

What Bryan didn't tell anyone was that the salary was only for the few months of football season and not the entire year.

Arrival

A lone figure stepped off the train and into the warm September night. Pulling down his top hat, he clasped his new waistcoat tighter to ward off the night air. A quick glance up and down the vacant platform revealed no welcoming committee, no brass bands. In truth, it revealed no one at all. After four days and five trains, this journey would end in darkness.

This was not the greeting Dietz had anticipated for the heralded arrival of the new Washington State College football coach.

Out of the void, a young man quietly approached this well-dressed stranger. It was Edgar Muir, the son of the livery stable owner. For two days, people had been waiting for their new football coach to arrive, but they had ended up leaving without reward. Only young Edgar took the time to check this one late train in the day.

Dietz smiled to himself. It was just some kind of mix-up. Soon, the two of them would be headed to the nearby boarding house where Dietz would stay. There was only one problem: a large pile of suitcases, trucks, and bags that Dietz had brought along. It would take two trips with the carriage. At the boarding house, the owner blanched at all the bags, saying, "There's not enough room in this entire house, let alone the room I have for Mr. Dietz." But young Edgar proved himself to be resourceful for his years. Unloading what he could, he put Dietz into the carriage along with the rest of the bags and headed up the hill to the college to see whether there was room to store a few bags at the Men's Gymnasium.

For Dietz, it was a chance to see his new town for the first time.

Pullman, Washington was only forty years old. Surrounded by miles of rolling wheat fields, the town had become a hub for commerce and was populated by a few hundred people with a reputation for being innovative and resourceful. It sat at the crossing of three railroads. When the Washington State Legislature announced plans to build a new land-grant college in 1889, Pullman's city leaders held a campaign that raised 160 acres for the cause. Their plan worked, and by 1892, the newly established Washington State College opened its doors to eighty-four students.

Into this collegiate environment stepped William Dietz, with the hopes of helping to rebuild a football team with a long tradition of losing. Looking about him, Dietz saw that a large mercantile store stood next to the livery stable. A small Western Union telegraph office squeezed in next door to a simple building marked with a sign reading "City Hall." Dietz glanced at his watch and realized it was after 11 p.m. No wonder the place was as quiet as a graveyard.

Rally

John Frederick Bohler, known to everyone as "Doc," had become the Washington State College's new Director of the Department of Physical Education and Athletics. A quiet man, with sandy-colored hair and blue eyes hidden behind round wire rim glasses, he saw athletics as a way to build strong minds as well as strong bodies. Hired on as a trainer and a coach a few years before, Bohler was that rare, natural leader with a strong knowledge of physical education theory. He also had the respect of athletes, having played center for the Reading Bears, a professional basketball team.

But Bohler had a big problem. While his school had hired a new football coach, the college was dangerously at risk of not having a team at all. After last year's dismal season, he knew it would be a challenge just to get players to come back to campus early, let alone finish out their college football careers. Bohler had a few creative ideas up his sleeve to reconnect with his players. Smiling, he had just wrapped up a package to his quarterback Arthur "Bull" Durham. The crafty quarterback was far up in the woods of northern Idaho logging. In the package were Durham's helmet and a new football. Bohler finished up the letter to Durham, saying, "Grab your helmet and make your way to Pullman soon. A new coach, and a new season; there is plenty for us to get excited about."

Satisfied with his choice, Bohler began writing his second letter to his captain, Asa "Ace" Clark, an older player who had been spending time working in the mines north of Spokane, but was now back working on his family's farm. Bohler hoped the delivery of a new football along with a jersey might help spark an early return to Pullman.

Impressions

It was Dietz's first morning in his new town. The time change and all of the excitement in getting here had been exhausting. As he began his first daylight venture through town, Dietz was certainly one to attract attention. His outgoing appearance and his flair for fashion gave him a purposeful look as he strolled around the town. Everything seemed all shiny and new to Dietz. The town had certainly been the benefactor of a nearby college. It was difficult to know where the town ended and the college boundaries began.

While he had hoped for an anonymous walk to campus, Dietz was surprised by the number of people who casually passed by with a welcome greeting. In this small town, the arrival of a new football coach brought with it a renewed sense of spirit and support for the football program. But Dietz was certainly one to make an impression. He knew winning over these local fans would be critical to the team's success. He told a reporter, "The first essential to turning out a good football team…is the undivided confidence of the people."

Dressed in his best coat and top hat, he paced himself up the hill, using a shiny walking stick. It would be his first day on the job, and his first chance to meet face to face with his new boss, President Enoch Bryan, who until today had only been a name on a contract. Their meeting would likely be without note, more of a formality.

Dietz was more eager for the team meeting awaiting him—as were his new players.

Team

"Doc" Bohler had worked his magic. Nearly two dozen players had answered the call to end their summer break early and return to school. The players gathered in the gym with the quiet excitement that greets most athletes before the season begins. The room was filled with the sounds of players renewing friendships and catching up on the months that had passed since their last connection. The new coach added a layer of optimism.

Standing at the door, Coach William Dietz gazed at the players in front of him as he began his own assessments. For the past few weeks, he had been pouring over player notes and game reviews to get a sense of what he had to work with. But this was his first chance to see the players themselves.

His first impressions were not good.

It didn't take an expert to understand why this team had not performed well the previous season. Around the room stood a gangly collection of young men, none over 180 pounds, with maybe two or three true athletes among them. If they looked more like a collection of farmers, ranchers, and laborers than athletes, there was a simple reason: they were.

But this was no time for second guesses. It was time for him to forge a connection between himself and his players. Before players will care to believe in what you do, they need to believe that you care for them as a team, even as individuals. Dietz knew his first impression was critical.

The meeting would be brief. There would be time in the days ahead to reveal all he would ask of them. Yet there would be one surprise at this first gathering. The team would not be in Pullman long. Dietz had made plans to take the players and coaches north, away from campus, where they could eat, sleep, and spend their entire time focusing on football. It was a strategy few teams had yet learned to adopt.

Dietz's last words at the meeting would be what players remembered the most. As he walked out the door, Dietz offered one promise: "Trust me on this; you will surprise a lot of teams this year. Of that you have my word."

CAMP

Liberty Lake
September 1915

There wasn't much to build on from the previous 1914 season.
That season had begun with the Washington State team dropping
its opener against a conglomerate of hand-picked players who
all played for the University of Montana (including, surprisingly,
two former Washington State players). The very next week
against Oregon, the team claimed somewhat of a victory, having
won the game, only to see its final touchdown reversed over a
questionable call from the referee. Fans regarded the next game
against the Oregon Agriculture College as one of the team's finest
performances. The team fought hard in hopes of at least a tie, only
to see it slip away in the final seconds because of a Washington State
fumble. A number of players had been seriously injured in that
game, including Captain Asa Clark, who suffered broken ribs, but
refused to be benched. The team's first victory came against Idaho,
a difficult 3-0 win. But then came the ugly season-ending contest
on Thanksgiving Day in Seattle. The final score was Washington
45, Washington State 0. The Washington State players knew the
lopsided game should have been much, much worse. Behind
the scenes, the 1914 team had faced tough challenges from the
beginning. No real sense of team had developed. The team lacked
the physical size needed to play competitive football. Opponents
on the schedule were filled with players topping 250 pounds.

Dietz believed a fresh start this year would do more than adjust the team to his new style of play. He needed to build a team that believed! Not just in the system, or the coach, but in themselves.

Captain-elect Asa Clark was sent to scout out a suitable location for a two-week camp. Early September made it easy to find openings, but Dietz had been very specific. He wanted Clark to find a lakeside resort with a large field for training, and it needed to be self-contained. So that first Monday in September, some twenty-two young men traveled north by train to Clark's top choice—a thirty-five-acre resort on the west side of Liberty Lake. The setting was ideally suited for young men who had just finished up a summer of hard work. It offered warm sun in the morning, but nearby hills cast an afternoon shade with a gentle cool breeze from the south. Each man would share a cottage with another. As the train pulled into the Liberty Lake campground, the players moved to the windows like eager school kids. Piling out, the group gathered outside the campground, waiting for assigned cabin space. Groans and moans began immediately as older players were assigned cabins at random with younger players.

What Bohler had pulled off in just a few weeks was nothing short of miraculous. He had arranged for a local farmer to round up fresh eggs, milk, cheese, and vegetables and bring them in every other day. He had even found a special cook to prepare the daily training table. Per Dietz's instructions, Bohler had also come up with everything from canoes to tennis racquets. The training schedule might have looked more like a vacation trip, but it was all part of Dietz's plan.

There wasn't much time. The opening game against Oregon was just over one month away.

Revelry

Clarence Zimmerman was the closest thing on the team to a typical football player. At 6'2" and weighing in just shy of 190, he was almost too big for the camping cot. The cabin had barely warmed to the morning sun when an enormous racket caused him to leap from his bed.

"Rise and shine! Rise and shine!" the voice sang out. Peeking outside, Zimmerman and others blinked to see new football coach Dietz clanging on a metal bucket with a wooden spoon. This would be their first morning under a new coach and a new system. Players turned out quickly, eager to make a good first impression. From the very beginning, it was clear this would be no ordinary training camp. Traditional calisthenics were followed by a robust team run through the nearby hills.

If Dietz had any concerns about the team before him, he kept them private. Some of the players looked as if they had worked heavy labor their entire lives: players like Asa Clark, who came back to college after spending years in the mines saving up money for college. Others, like the Hanley brothers, looked as if they had just left high school. Dick Hanley was the older of the two, a scrappy Irishman said to be the best fighter on campus. The younger Leroy Hanley shared many of the same characteristics. Both shared a true love of the game's intricacies.

Arthur Durham, known by the nickname "Bull," was a versatile athlete and a hands-on favorite to be quarterback. A natural leader, he rarely spoke, but when he did, people took notice. Similar in personality was Alfred Langdon, a quiet, lanky man from a nearby small-town farm who dreamed of seeing the world he had only read about in books. Harry "Hack" Applequist had been raised on an apple farm in central Washington and had worked for several years after high school to save up enough money for college. Geology was his love.

After a tough morning workout, the team was greeted in the dining hall by an amazing array of smells. Roasted meats, fresh vegetables and fruits, and sweetbreads were all served alongside trays of different types of cheese and pitchers of cold milk. It was a king's feast—the likes of which many of these players had never experienced. These were small-town young men, raised by hard-working farm families who survived by living only on what they needed. The idea of serving up such an extravagance would have never occurred to them. Behind the serving table was Coach Dietz himself, who ensured each player would receive a healthy portion.

The late afternoons were given over to leisure activity. One such afternoon, Arthur Durham was found toying with a chess set in the main hall. Durham, too, had taken a few years off to work on the farm and save enough money for college. For two years, he had started as quarterback. But Durham had developed another skill. He could drop-kick a football some 45 yards. Unfortunately, it was a skill he rarely used. His team rarely got close enough for him to try.

When Dietz came upon Arthur, he offered to play him. Sitting across from Durham, he set down a chess timer, a bit of a surprise in this lakeside resort, given that they were rarely used. Dietz suggested they make the game more interesting by giving each player only thirty seconds per move.

Durham always loved the analytical side of playing chess. He loved the strategy, and loved examining every option. But this game Dietz was proposing was something different. Little did Durham realize this simple strategy was part of Dietz's plan....

Meanwhile, walking by himself outside, Asa Clark, the most senior statesman on this team, carried an external sense of confidence that hid self-doubt. At twenty-eight, Clark was older than most of his classmates, an age difference that had kept him away from many social activities. Clark, known on the team as "Ace," had played backup running back the previous year and was hoping to land a place as a starter his senior year. Like many young men, Clark too was trying to find his way. His family's farm was very small. Their one-room house still had a dirt floor. Running water was something that happened in the city. Yet any thought of farm or family or even graduation took a back seat here at camp. Clark's mind was focused on football and how to convince this new coach it should be his day to shine.

Clark and the others found themselves incredibly busy, with one activity leading right into the next. First, the lake offered everything from swim meets to canoe racing. The nearby mountains were the scene of leisurely hikes and long runs, plenty of runs. On the training field, the emphasis was on technique. As the days continued, many, like Clark, began to ask, "When are we going to play football?" But in truth, Dietz was preparing them for something different. The cross-training built strength, while the playfulness of the day developed camaraderie.

The first sign of any connections had formed came with the emergence of nicknames for nearly every player.

Arthur Durham was called Bull by his teammates. Some insisted it was because he was bull-headed. Others declared it was the way he moved his head back and forth when he crashed through the line. More likely, his nickname came from the popular tobacco of the day named "Bull Durham." The quarterback had been among the first players Bohler had lured back to school.

Carl Dietz, who often joked that Coach Dietz was his uncle, instantly became known as "Red" because of his flaming red hair. It was a name he eagerly accepted because he hated his other nickname of "Keyhole." That name came when Carl returned to the dorm after curfew late one night and spent more than an hour in the dark, trying to find the lock to let him inside. As for the rest of the players, most were given nicknames that used portion of their names, such as "Bangs" for Benton Bangs, the running back, a relief to him after the coach had intervened and rejected nicknames related to his reputation as a "ladies man."

One by one, Dietz learned each player's story, which revealed more than just his name and position. Slowly, the nucleus of a team began to form and key questions were answered for Dietz, such as: "Who are the leaders?" "Who has the most drive and determination?" and "Whom do I need to win over to make this team a success?"

So far, he liked what he was seeing.

One evening, Dietz decided it was time to reveal something of himself. "Gentlemen, I have a simple philosophy; the only labels that count are the ones you place on yourself. You might look at me and see a man who is part Indian. But when I look in the mirror, all I see is a man."

Dietz went on to tell how his true name was *Wicarhpi Isnala,* a Sioux Indian name that translated means "Lone Star." He then related the remarkable story of his family. "My father was an engineer from Germany, brought over to this country to help build the railroad. One year as winter began, he was out on a two-day scouting mission for a new route when his camp was overrun by warring factions of young men from nearby tribes of Northern Cheyenne, Sioux, and Arapaho. When my father returned, the camp was empty. No supplies. No tents. No horses. Facing certain starvation in the winter months, my father decided to follow the survivors' tracks to find safety. Instead, he followed the wrong tracks and found himself right in the middle of the Sioux nation."

It was a riveting tale. Coach Dietz recalled the story from deep within his memory, as if this were a tale not often told. "My father threw himself on the mercy of the tribe. The chief was so taken by this act of bravery that he took my father in. My mother was assigned to teach him their language. They would fall in love and be married. Some years after, I was born; my father decided we should move back to what he called 'civilization.' But life can be rough as a child for someone who is half-white and half-Sioux. Neither side fully accepts you."

Dietz's players knew the story spoke volumes about the man in front of them.

But not one to dwell on the past, Dietz soon set aside the storytelling to engage them in a simple counting game he called "Stomp." Simple enough, the leader would call out a number, usually from one to five, and the rest of the players would then "stomp" their feet in unison before ending in a clap. For example, if the number were three, then the rest of the team would respond with a "stomp, stomp clap." It seemed like a simple game, but it was one that became complex as the coach called out new numbers in rapid succession. It seemed a silly game to end the day, yet without realizing it, the team had just learned one of Dietz's most important lessons: how to respond to a snap count together at the same time.

Day Two and More

While the first few days were filled with more leisure activities than football training, the team got a glimpse of Coach Dietz's system with the introduction of another new game. It would be a relay race across the parade ground where the players were required to jump face-first across a log, tuck in their shoulders, hit the ground, and roll back up onto their feet in full stride. Two logs had been placed length-wise across the practice field. Players could either roll with their left or right shoulder. The hardest part would be learning how to tuck in one's head.

At first, the drill was frustrating. It didn't make much sense to the players. That is until Dietz explained its purpose. He called it "the rolling block." The concept was simple. Players would drop down to make a block in an open field by "rolling" into the opponent's legs; roll underneath, then jump back up, looking for another man to block. It was a difficult concept to grasp. But it would be the first technique Dietz would instill from his days back at Carlisle.

For the first few days, players began to wonder whether they were ever going to play football. There was plenty of time spent on leisurely walks, enjoying the coolness of the lake, even playing baseball. Instead, the team found itself running—and running plenty. There were sprints, afternoon jogs, even relay races. It wasn't until well into the camp that the team saw the first glimpse of their new football scheme.

As the players gathered for an evening meal, the coach revealed his strategy. Using a chalkboard, Dietz fell back on the traditional method of writing out plays using Xs and Os. His scheme would be quite different. Instead of having a traditional backfield with two halfbacks, a fullback, and a quarterback, Dietz would split out one or both of the backs to the side. At first glance, players wondered whether this would be within the rules, but Dietz insisted that by lining a "wing" off the line of scrimmage, they would essentially remain running backs.

Among the most startling revelations was when Dietz split his players up into two camps of offense and defense. Their entire lives these young men had been used to a game where players stayed on the field the entire game. Under the Dietz plan, players would rotate in, keeping them fresh on every play. If the coach were eager to implement his system quickly, it didn't show. Perhaps he'd learned his patience from his mentor, Pop Warner, who believed true change was made by evolution, not revolution. Dietz knew he needed to build this team one element at a time.

It's one thing to see a strategy on paper or a chalkboard. It's quite another to see it in action. Among the first plays the team walked through would be a new concept Dietz called "the pulling lineman," a strange concept at first, but one that began to build excitement in the team. The idea was first born at Carlisle. When the ball was snapped, the plan was to have a lineman step backwards, then turn and sprint down the line of scrimmage. It was a way for the team to add an extra player into a sweep. It wouldn't be easy. A lineman would need to be fast enough to outrun his backfield ahead of the sweep. But under the plan, five blockers would be ahead on one ball carrier sprinting outside. Add in a rolling block and these strategies began to build excitement among the players. Especially when Dietz revealed it was this very strategy that Carlisle had used so effectively in knocking off much larger and stronger teams such as Penn State.

As the team wrapped up for the day, Dietz caught up with his elder player, Asa Clark. "Ace, can I have a word with you?" Clark stopped.

Dietz told Clark a story about his playing days at Carlisle. Dietz had been the running back until a new player, Jim Thorpe, came on the scene. But Pop Warner had an idea. He would drop Dietz down as a lineman since Dietz had the strength and speed to make the pulling lineman plan work.

Now it would be Dietz, the coach, asking the same of Asa Clark.

"Clark, I need you. Please don't tell anyone, but you are the one person on this team I need the most," said Dietz. "I need you to be my team leader. Someone I can count on to lead the men. Can I count on you?" Dietz paused, waiting for a response. Clark nodded his agreement.

Clark would also be one of a few players who would play both offense and defense. There was a reason his players had elected him as their captain.

Last Days

Clarence Zimmerman woke up smiling. The usual sound of clanging and banging on pots that had so profoundly disturbed him in previous days had been replaced with the sound of sticks striking each other along with the sounds of the coaches calling players to the day. There would be no more banging of the pots and pans to wake the team up. Someone had hidden them away.

The call to scrimmage was answered in the final days of camp. No more canoeing or leisurely walks in the woods. All the emphasis on conditioning soon became clear. Dietz planned on running plays together in rapid succession.

Coach Dietz loved the progress his team was making. With each new day, a real team was emerging. With camp wrapping up, Dietz told a reporter the players leaving the Liberty Lake camp were "as good a material as I ever saw."

More importantly, the players were showing signs of real teamwork.

The formula was a simple one steeped in the oldest of Sioux traditions. Build strength in the body, the heart, and the mind. Set the warriors' minds toward a singular goal. Turn their eyes inward to find their own strengths. Then turn them outward together as a single unit toward a common foe.

Duplicity Speaks

University of Washington President Henry Suzzallo was taking his fight into Washington's agricultural heartland in a bid to strip Washington State College of its science funding. In speeches and an interview with the Spokane newspaper, Suzzallo outlined his vision of a strong university for advanced education and a strong agricultural college. He wanted to limit instruction at the latter, claiming that having a state support two universities would result in having only two mediocre schools at best. In other words, limit what classes Washington State could teach.

Speaking before leaders from central Washington, Suzzallo made his boldest proposal to date, one he intended to take to the legislature. Suzzallo intended to ask that 100,000 acres of land originally deeded to Washington State College as part of its land-grant mission be put into the care and custody of the University of Washington for the purpose of creating one great scientific institution.

As if that weren't enough, he was asking lawmakers to divorce any notion of science from Washington State College.

RETURN TO PULLMAN

September 1915

An energized group of men returned from camp to Pullman with a renewed spirit and a new sense of pride. Dietz had made it clear the players would need to look the part of a successful football team, so on the Friday before every game and at team events when they traveled, players would be required to wear their best suits. Dietz believed the best way to begin thinking like a champion was to dress like one.

A hot August morning greeted the team, standing in their familiar wool pants and leather helmets, for that first official practice. The final days of camp had been filled with the team running play after play in rapid succession. As quickly as they finished one play, Dietz had lined them up for another. It became clear why Dietz had them running so early in the camp. One last difference that bothered the players was a lack of scrimmaging. As practice now began here in Pullman, many hoped it would offer the chance to get back in the trenches and play the game.

The Dietz strategy would prove to be one far different from what these players had long known. The "dive-block" had proven to be a difficult technique to master. As they began to learn the new offensive schemes, an entirely new level of deception was needed—one that had seemed easy when first learned at a slow speed, but one that was difficult to perfect on a dead run. In many ways, Dietz had introduced a completely different game than the one many had enjoyed since before high school.

But class was far from over. Dietz continued to offer surprises.

On offense, he wanted to get rid of the huddle.

The Chessboard

On a lazy hot afternoon at camp, Arthur Durham had first learned of this new concept. It seemed strange to him at first, but easier to master than the game of chess. It began when Coach Dietz had introduced a chess timer to their afternoon game. A quicker game, Dietz had suggested, would make things "more interesting." It was one thing to play a game of chess at a leisurely pace, quite another to make calculated moves in under five seconds.

It was during one of these afternoon sessions that Dietz first offered a revolutionary concept to his quarterback. Instead of gathering the players huddling together on offense, Dietz explained how the quarterback would signal the next play as players lined up. With a whisper here or a hand gesture there, the offense would be ready on the line of scrimmage before the defense ever had a chance to set up. For Durham, it meant the game of football would now be played one, two, even three plays ahead. Now it became clear why the team had played the game of "Stomp." Players needed to think in unison in order to drive off the ball as one.

Durham had to shake his head. This would be a new game for him. Not only would calling plays fall on his shoulders, but in many formations, he would actually be a blocker. Even the most basic of quarterback techniques would not be used in the Dietz system. The lanky Alfred Langdon had become the newest center because of his ability to "long-snap" the ball. No more would the quarterback be the first to touch the ball from the center. Instead, the ball would be snapped back to any player in the backfield some fifteen feet behind the line of scrimmage.

Final Days

The players had a lot of changes to absorb.

On this first day of official practice, the coach decided to keep things simple. Asa Clark lined up in his new spot at guard. Bull Durham stepped in as quarterback. Carl Dietz lined up in the fullback spot, with Benton Bangs at halfback. Hack Applequist took his familiar place at left tackle. Clarence Zimmerman lined up as the end on the right. Dick Hanley was moved into the new "wing" position just outside Zimmerman on the right, but 1 yard off the line of scrimmage. The rest of the players gathered around to watch how it would all come together.

Instead of using a traditional system of numbers and formations, Dietz lined up his players and gave the plays a name. Grabbing his lineman Hack Applequist by the arm, Dietz walked the team through how the lineman would pull out ahead of the play. "Hack here will be the star. In his honor, we'll call this 'Apple,'" said Dietz. Should the play go the other way, it would be called the "Clark." The team chuckled at the idea that a lineman would be leading the play. What Dietz next described would be a ballet of motion. As the ball was snapped, Applequist would take a step backwards, then sprint to the right. To buy him time, Durham would grab the ball out of the air and then take a step to the left, as if the team were heading the other way. Both backs would do the same thing. This simple move was brilliant by design. It would shift the defense in the wrong direction while buying Applequist time to get to the other side. The backs would then plant that first step and drive themselves in the other direction.

Ready to try this new play out, players lined up with the quarterback, Durham, standing back behind his center; he called out a familiar snap cadence of "hut-hut-hike." On the snap, Hack stood up and shot to his right. Durham took the ball, backed out like he was running left, and then switched his step to the other direction. In unison, the backfield did the same maneuver. With Carl leading the way, Durham handed the ball to Bangs who followed right behind. The players all joined together behind Hack Applequist, who led the charge against an imaginary set of defenders.

Walking over to Dick Hanley, Dietz explained how the wing back now gave this scheme an added advantage. The end would be blocking from the outside in. His job would be to come crashing down on the first defender to clear the line of scrimmage. Walking through this play again and again, it became clear that it would not be so easy to master.

Following the Carlisle tradition, Dietz would only install a handful of plays. Along the way, different variations would be added. Adding to the simplicity, Dietz would have his quarterback add the snap count to the call. The challenge was to make sure everyone heard the play call as he quickly approached the line. "Apple-three" was what the quarterback Durham would whisper to the team. It meant they would snap the ball on three, with Applequist leading the charge around the line. As time passed, the team would also work on calling several plays in a row. With a snap, center Alfred Langdon would get the ball into the hands of the running back, eliminating the handoff entirely.

In just two weeks, Dietz had changed every facet of their game.

Defense

With Dietz teaching the offense, the defensive duties landed squarely on Doc Bohler. It was hard to convince players to sit out half the game, but the idea of using this extra energy certainly had its advantages. The key to this defensive scheme was for players to be as confusing as possible to the other team. Traditionally, a football team's defense had already lined up when the offense came to the line of scrimmage. Under the Dietz/Bohler plan, defenders would be constantly on the move right up until the moment the ball was snapped. The rules stated you only had to have three linemen in a down and set position when the ball was snapped. The rules didn't say what could happen before.

The Washington State defense would have its own names for plays. One of the highlights of the last season had been when the tall Clarence Zimmerman had intercepted a pass against Idaho. It was somewhat of a fluke, but from it was born a defensive strategy. It began with Zimmerman left unblocked on a play—not uncommon when the offense is running to the opposite side of the field. Faked into thinking it was a run in the other direction, the lanky lineman stood straight up, looking for the play as it moved away. That's when a crossing end for Idaho cut behind him, waving for the ball. Zimmerman's arms shot up in somewhat of a defensive surprise, like a forward playing basketball. He, along with everyone else in the stadium, could hardly believe his luck when his extra-long arms knocked the ball out of the air and down into his hands. Linemen so rarely get a chance to touch the ball. Zimmerman reacted like a surge of adrenaline had jolted his body. Newspaper writers would say he grabbed the ball like a hungry bear, lumbering up the field before being taken down from behind.

From that one play, assistant coach Doc Bohler saw an opportunity to develop a strategy in which a wide receiver would be left alone intentionally in the area where he would catch a short pass, as if the covering defender had chosen to come after the quarterback instead. Calling it the "Zimmerman," the play was actually a deception where, at the last minute, the tall lineman would stand up and run backwards into the passing lane. A safety would be available to cover the receiver should they decide to try a long pass.

In the days ahead, Doc would also work to design defensive plays to confuse the offense. One of the most popular was what he called "Log-jam." Bohler knew his Washington State players couldn't stand up to the power teams that used men half-again as large to push a wall of force down the field. Log-jam lined up defensive players both inside and outside the tackles and then pinched everything toward the middle. Inside linemen would shoot into the gaps, staying low to prevent players from driving with their feet. The resulting action was a giant "log-jam" of players that would make it nearly impossible for the running backs to do anything but go around. The team was counting on the fresh legs of its speedy linebackers and defensive backs to close up the distance. The concept was simple: let the offense gain 1 to 3 yards on any play, but keep them from making it the full 10 yards for a first down.

For those watching from the sidelines, this defense must have seemed bizarre to watch. Players would line up in strange formations. Five people would pack together on one side, only to move around constantly until the ball was snapped. Linemen would go backwards into new positions. Defensive backs would get a three-step jump and fill their places. "Jumping beans" became the best description of their movements, a take-off of the popular children's toy. To the outside observer, it must have seemed like the defense was wasting a lot of energy before the ball was even snapped. But the coaches were hoping it was a dance that would confuse the offense enough to give their team the edge.

Pullman

The beginning of any sporting season is filled with optimism. For these players returning back to Pullman, there was an added dimension: a hunger for success. The time away had been filled non-stop with activities, new plays, and constant training. Back on campus, the everyday pace of school would return with hopes that what the team had learned in camp would not be forgotten.

Officially, this would be the first public practice, bringing a renewed sense of enthusiasm. Several reporters were on hand to talk with Dietz, along with a few fans. It was a different atmosphere than the players had ever seen before. The added attention, the heat (temperatures in the low 90s), and the pressure of implementing a new system would sometimes flow over into frustration. After one failed play, quarterback Bull Durham let his emotions get the best of him; he took a few steps away from the team, and on the move, promptly drop-kicked the football through the goal posts some 35 yards away.

The kick caught the eye of Coach Dietz.

The "drop-kick" is one of the most difficult plays in all of football. The rules state the ball must be on the ground before it is kicked for any extra point or field goal to count. A rare athlete could drop the ball like a punt, and then kick it just as it touched the ground. Not only had Durham just drop-kicked the ball from 35 yards out, but he had done it while on the run.

Smiling, Dietz walked across the field to his quarterback. The coach had just learned he had a new weapon in his offensive arsenal.

Enlisting Help

As the players headed to the locker room after practice, Coach Dietz walked up behind Clarence Zimmerman and asked him for a word. With a few players walking away still in earshot, Coach Dietz said, "Zim, I'm thinking of having you spend some time on both sides of the ball, offense and defense. It won't be easy. You'll need to get together with Doc to learn his defensive schemes." Zimmerman wasn't surprised. He had played both ways since he first learned the game.

If Zim had any hesitation, it was because this new game Dietz had designed had a lot of things to learn, let alone master. Leaning in, Dietz spoke in a quieter, almost familiar tone. "Zim, I'm going to level with you. I need you. Don't tell the other players, but you are the one I need to count on the most to lead this team." Smiling now, Dietz said, "Let's keep this just between you and me," and with that, Dietz turned to walk back to his office.

Newspaper Clip

Pullman Herald, September 1915

> With the ability of the majority of the big contingent of new men still a matter of conjecture, it appears that Coach William Dietz, new football mentor at Washington State College, will have an abundance of backfield men in his squad, but will be somewhat weak on line material, and a strong line is the first essential to a successful team, according to the deductions of the Carlisle man.

> Coach Dietz is using the pass entirely, Center Langdon passing directly to the man who is to carry the ball.

> Local football fans will have an opportunity to see the new and unproven material in actual play for the first time Wednesday afternoon, when the annual Freshman-Sophomore game will be staged.

Freshman-Sophomore Competition

The freshman-sophomore competition was a fall ritual played out every year at Washington State College. It involved a bold competition to see which class could "catch" the largest number of freshman or sophomore men, tie them up, and bring them to the football field for counting. The event kicked off a week of activities designed to see which of the two younger classes could claim superiority over the other. It had been a simpler game in the early years when there were only a handful of new students. But with over 1,600 students on campus, the hunting of male first- and second-year students had become a full-fledged sporting event.

In preparing for it, classes issued "proclamations," such as banning freshmen from wearing anything with a high school insignia or not allowing them to bring a "date" to any sporting event. Townspeople were issued warnings so that the kidnapping of students from a city street would not cause any witnesses undue stress. Because of the large numbers, college administrators limited the "hunting season" to between 4:30 and 7:30 p.m. Hundreds of spectators would line the area to see who might bring in the most "game." Electric lights were rigged to help fans see well.

But this year, about one hundred members of the freshman class decided there was strength in numbers, so they marched to the football field en masse. Having tied up some seventeen sophomores, the class circled around them, issuing taunts and jeers to their captured clan. With time running out, it appeared the freshmen would carry the day. With only fifteen minutes to go, their celebrations were frozen when an even larger contingent of sophomores rolled over the hillside like an angry hoard. Adding to the confusion, someone decided to turn off the lights. A few cars around the stadium switched on their headlights to try to offer some clarity to the onlookers.

As the lights came back on, witnesses saw a large scale "donnybrook" being waged between hundreds of young men, fighting hand-to-fist in an attempt to capture and "tie-up" as many of their opponents as possible. A large cloud of dust soon emerged from the battle. A few of the co-eds had slipped into the fray themselves, working to untie their classmates.

Judges didn't know how to stop the violence, until one of the referees borrowed a pistol and fired it into the air at 7:30, causing the fight to end almost instantly. Many of the young men collapsed to the ground, exhausted from fighting. Despite the disturbance, the counting began. This round would go to the freshman class. Final tally: 77 to 33.

Freshman-Sophomore Game

On Wednesday, the older classmen came to assist with the annual freshman-sophomore game, where the squad was divided into two teams with the younger players getting the starring role. The idea had been the brainchild of the previous head coach John Bender, who wanted to offer the younger players a chance to show what they could do. In truth, the younger players had very little chance of making the varsity squad, but many of them would help by serving on the practice squad against the varsity—an important role since they would work to emulate the offense and defense of the next opponent to help better prepare the starters on the field.

Dietz was watching over preparations when he felt a tap on his shoulder. It was his assistant coach Tommy Tyrer. Alongside Tyrer was a young freshman he wanted Dietz to meet—Ronald Fishback. It was easy to see why Tyrer had brought him forward for a personal introduction. Fishback stood 6'2" and weighed 210 pounds. Easily, he was one of the largest men on the field. A football player in high school, Fishback had also been a state contender in the 100-yard dash. Fast—his time of 10.1 seconds placed him among the fastest athletes in the country. College sports shunned allowing freshmen to play on the varsity teams, but not Dietz. Fishback might make the varsity team without even trying out.

As the freshman-sophomore game began, the biggest surprise was the turnout. Some fifty new athletes were on the field in hopes of catching the coach's eye. It was a moment of fun for the juniors and seniors who helped in the coaching. But their respite would be short-lived. Practice was scheduled immediately after the game. For the varsity, their first big test would be on Saturday for the annual Alumni Game. Doc Bohler had been busy recruiting a number of former players, with hopes of giving the team what Coach Dietz wanted—a real battle with a chance to see just how this team would perform with a new system and possibly a new attitude. Bohler would also play.

Duplicity Continues

The University of Washington campaign had taken on a new public face. In a speech in nearby Spokane, President Henry Suzzallo told a group of leaders "None of your sons or daughters even *go* to Washington State College."

In truth, over 900 of Washington State's students were from Spokane.

For WSC President Bryan, the campaign had begun to test his resolve. How could a college separate out the sciences and still be an effective institution of higher education? Of greater concern, the issue was now gaining traction in the Washington state legislature.

Bryan's days were filled with writing letters, giving testimony, and urging lawmakers to consider a new approach. The war for validation was being waged in full.

ALUMNI GAME

Pullman, Washington
September 1915

A downpour of rain, driven by a surprising September wind, greeted the two teams meeting for the annual Washington State College alumni game. The Washington State players found themselves pacing around, nervous about this first gridiron test. Hundreds of fans had already gathered in the stands to see what this new coach and his new team had to offer. If Coach Dietz had any concerns, they didn't show. He casually strolled along the sideline, talking to players individually with a relaxed demeanor, not typical of football coaches of the day.

Across the way, the alumni players began to filter in. Doc Bohler had put together a pretty outstanding team. Bohler himself would play the game and would be filling in as quarterback and defensive back. Joining him were Dietz's two assistant coaches. Tommy Tyrer looked eager to get back into the game. After all, the four-time, all-conference end had been training right alongside the team and felt prepared. The other assistant coach, Eddie Kienholz, was no slouch either. As a two-way lineman, he had earned a letter in all four years. Joining the team were also a few players with rather "loose" ties to the college. The biggest surprise was two large imposing players from the championship Montana team. Bohler learned they were on campus after having spent the summer attending a Washington State College class in veterinary medicine not offered by their school.

If Dietz wanted a challenge, he would get it—a jumbo-sized one at that.

To make the game as real as possible, there would be a running clock. Two regional referees were on hand as well, having worked the popular Pullman versus Palouse High School game the night before. The biggest difference was that Coach Dietz would be alone on the sideline since his assistant coaches were all lined up on the other side of the field. Doc Bohler and his two assistants walked across the field for the coin toss. Dietz was joined by his captain, Asa Clark, and his quarterback, Arthur Durham. Dietz had pledged to the players that the second captain spot would be claimed by the player who showed the most leadership in camp. The team had almost unanimously supported Durham.

A long evening of rain had taken its toll on the field. Already, water was pooling up under the players' feet. Special game boots with cleats were leaking water, despite being rubbed down the night before with mink oil. The players met at mid-field for the coin toss. The conference referee seemed eager to get things underway since the rains threatened to grow heavier. "Gentlemen, we will be following all of the regular rules of collegiate football this afternoon. Two thirty-minute halves, being controlled now by the large clock hanging on the announcer's box," he said, pointing to the clock above the home field sideline. "Mr. Tyrer, as the visiting captain, please signify your choice." Tyrer said, "Tails."

The coin was tossed into the air and landed in the mud with a splash. Bending down, the referee declared, "It is tails. Alumni, will you kick or receive?" With a touch of bravado, Tyrer replied, "We'll take the ball in the second half." Deferring the kick was something only done when you believed your defense was far superior to the opposing team's offense. For Dietz, this would be a true test of his ideas and his coaching. It was Bohler's job to provide the challenge.

Kick-Off

Benton Bangs would be the first to the touch the ball in the new Dietz football era. The high, lazy kick-off floated down to the 30-yard line as the thundering line of alumni came crashing ahead. But Bangs' time with the football was short-lived; the wet leather ball slipped out of his hands almost as soon as he got his hands on it. Chasing the ball madly, Bangs finally managed to fall onto the ball. A mountain of players piled on top ensured he would not have the chance to bounce up and recover.

Bangs had barely stood up when he realized the offense was ready to go. Most of the players from the offensive unit were already on the field and well-practiced in the art of speedy recovery. Bangs had just handed off the ball to the referee when quarterback Bull Durham whispered into his helmet "Apple-3." Durham and Clark had worked on a new plan where the quarterback would tell the lineman the play, and they would in turn tell the rest of the players. "Apple" was the name of the first sweep to the right that the team had ever invented. "3" meant the call would be snapped on the third count. The referee was caught by surprise as he set the ball and prepared to blow his whistle, signaling the clock should start. As the referee turned from placing the ball, the Washington State College team was already over it. The referee shrugged his shoulders; when looking over to the defense, he saw the Alumni team was also ready to begin. Coach Doc Bohler had seen to it that his defenders would be ready for this new level of play.

Bangs, now from his backfield position, heard Durham call out, "Hut-hut-hike!" In the excitement, Langdon put a bit more snap on the ball than he should and the ball nearly sailed over Bangs' head. He reached up and managed to grab the ball. Ahead, he saw only chaos. While Durham pretended to catch the ball and sprint left, everyone else was blocking down to the right. Not fooled by any of this misdirection, defenders were heading straight for him. Bangs quickly sidestepped his first rusher and then plowed into the line in hopes of pushing himself into the defense. Gaining about 3 yards, Bangs was dropped under a pile of defenders. By the time he got untangled, the offense was already set and ready to go. Passing by his waiting quarterback, he heard the exact same call "Apple-3."

For Bangs, this was going to be a long game.

By design, Durham was going to call the exact same play three successive times. The key difference would be in how Durham the quarterback would react. On the first play, he faked a carry to the left. It didn't work. The second play didn't fool the defense either. The line from Washington State had trouble holding back the larger linemen from Montana. Everything seemed to get disrupted. Applequist couldn't quite get past the mess to get outside and block. Langdon, the center, now had a man lined up directly on him who seemed intent to push him down on every snap. Again, the play ended with defenders slowing down play by piling onto Bangs.

On third down and 7 yards to go, the defense seemed to open up just enough that the simplicity of the Dietz game took hold. Applequist shot to his right and quickly dropped to seal off the pressing lineman. This gave Bangs the avenue he needed to sprint around the corner. The younger Hanley came down on the sliding linebacker—not only stopping him, but creating a jam that slowed other players in pursuit. The opening was all Bangs needed. Dropping his head, he burst into full speed, quickly gaining the first down and showing no signs of stopping. As a pursuing defensive back angled to catch the wily back, Bangs tried to switch the ball to his left hand. That's when the slick football shot out of his grasp. One of the Alumni defensive backs dropped onto the ball, and just like that, the first series of the new Washington State college offense would end in a turnover. Bangs stopped and looked straight into the air in frustration. With the defensive unit coming onto the field, Bangs slowly angled over to the sidelines, ready for the lecture he was sure would come.

But that lecture never happened.

Instead, Coach Dietz was busy talking with another player about his blocking technique. Bangs could only stand quietly, waiting for the expected wrath of an upset coach, but his wait would be short-lived. A cheer erupted from the dwindling number of onlookers as the Alumni team fumbled the ball, giving State a chance to redeem itself. As the defense came back to the sideline, one player who wouldn't stop grinning was Washington State's newest player, Ronald Fishback. The freshman had notched three tackles and had been in the Alumni backfield on several key plays.

With a chance for redemption, Washington State eagerly lined up to try again. But the second chance ended much like the first. Center Langdon snapped the ball too early, allowing the defense to bust into the line well before the offense was ready. Fullback Carl Dietz, who was supposed to take the ball up the middle, could only grab the ball in mid-air and push his way into the pile.

Quarterback Durham had seen the defense on the left side cheating over a bit and decided on the next play to snag the ball for himself. It was an option he had worked out with Coach Dietz that might give him the ball in open space with a head of steam, while his blockers would be heading in the other direction. As the team lined up, Durham grinned when the left linebacker shifted inside, allowing the other linebackers to cheat to the right. On the snap, the entire State team took off in its familiar sweep. The Alumni defense, coached well in advance by Bohler, had moved that direction to meet the threat. When Durham grabbed the ball out of the air, he shot to the left without a player in sight between him and the goal line some 80 yards away. Breaking around the corner, Durham turned his speed on full. Glancing right, two defenders were on their way, but it would be a race to the corner. After a 30-yard gain, Durham tried to sidestep them at the last instant. One missed, but the other made good, pushing him out-of-bounds. Quickly, Durham popped up, eager to get the next play going.

The rest of the team had already arrived when Durham called out to them "Apple-1!" Players had lined up and were ready to launch as the defenders were rushing to back onside. "Hut!" called out Durham. Bangs grabbed the handoff and raced around the right side for a solid 9 yards before being brought down by a combination of wet grass and the outstretched arm of a linebacker pushing his way past the blocking lineman, Asa Clark. Quickly, the Washington State team bounced back up, ready to go. Washington State was working to change the tempo of the game to one the defense wasn't quite ready to match.

On the next play, Bangs came crashing into the middle, following a familiar onslaught of blockers. But the wily veterans from Montana pulled an old trick—with the first player to reach Bangs grabbing him around the waist and standing him up while the second and third players batted at the ball. In an instant, the ball hit the ground where Doc Bohler, playing on the Alumni team, dropped on top of it. Almost as one voice, the offense collectively complained to the referee about the play, but to no avail. Feeling the game shift, the offense was eager to press on. But the fumble meant they would turn over the ball a mere 7 yards from the goal.

The game continued as a back-and-forth contest until partway into the second quarter, the rains began to fall so heavily that spectators could barely see across the field to the other side. Bad weather and a slow game had many of the fans headed for drier conditions. The referee pulled Dietz aside to ask whether he wanted to continue. Dietz was determined to see it through. "It's not as if this is the last time we'll face bad weather," said Dietz, adding with a twinkle in his eyes, "But if you want to let the clock run and not stop it down between plays, we might get out of here faster."

As the team rallied to the field for the second half, Dietz stopped Alfred Langdon on the way out. Dietz wanted his center to fire off the ball and drive his head into the nose tackle's chest, limiting how well the defender could react. Pulling him in close, the coach added,

"Alfred, the team needs you right now to be the leader." In an almost secretive manner, Dietz finished by saying, "Let's keep this just between you and me; what do you say?"

Second Half

The second half looked a lot like the first, with neither side able to move the ball well on the muddy ground. Nor was either able to hold onto the football very well. Late in the third quarter, the State team finally seemed to click together. Whether it was Alumni's first-game jitters, or a tired defense, State moved the ball efficiently down the field for one solid drive. Coming up a bit short, Durham called the pass option play. It meant that Zimmerman would go out for a pass, with everyone else staying in the block. If he were open, it would be a touchdown. If not, Durham would boot his now famous drop-kick.

From the snap, it was clear Zimmerman wasn't going anywhere. Two defensive players came slamming down onto the end, effectively buttoning him in, thanks to some insider coaching advice from Doc Bohler. With seeming ease, Durham dropped back and popped a 23-yard field goal to put the State team up 3-0.

The series gave the players a glimmer of hope. But that glimmer was soon dashed as the Alumni team returned the ensuing kick-off 80 yards to the Washington State 20-yard line. Unfazed, Dietz rotated in new linemen to keep them fresh. Sending his defense into the gaps between the Alumni linemen still kept creating havoc. It was almost a surprise when the final gun sounded. The referee had kept true to his word to speed up the game if the weather stayed wet. Both teams met in the middle of the field, with the two Montana players offering up the most praise. But despite their encouraging words, the State team headed dejectedly to the locker room. This was a game that the varsity would typically win by thirty or more points. Sure, they had won 3-0 on the scoreboard, but few felt like celebrating this victory. The next game they faced would be against a real opponent when the season began.

Team Meeting

Inside the locker room, the team sat waiting for the harsh words that come from a coach when a team doesn't perform. Many felt they had let the coach down. No one seemed eager to get out of his clothing. The silence met Coach Dietz as he walked inside. Players braced themselves for the yelling and angry words that were sure to come at any moment.

But that moment never happened.

Pausing briefly, Coach Dietz offered up only one comment, "We have plenty of work to do." Then he asked for the team to show up the next day at 6 a.m. With that, Dietz walked out the door, leaving behind a rather stunned room full of players.

A New Dawn

The next morning, the sun was still behind the horizon as the players gathered on the same football field where the game had been fought the day before. Clear skies were now breaking, with little evidence of the heavy rains the day before. Whatever emotions the players felt, few spoke openly about the game. The only thing missing was Coach Dietz.

As the sun began to rise, Clarence Zimmerman noticed something strange on the hill to the east. A lone figure stood with his back to the field, and he was wearing some kind of funny coat. With the sunlight bringing clarity with every new moment, it became clear this mysterious figure was, in fact, a man, standing with his arms folded and wearing a Sioux tribal outfit complete with war bonnet, a band of feathers that draped around the crown, and tanned leather with detailed markings and beadwork.

It was Coach Dietz.

Slowly, the team made its way toward this figure, gathering quietly, not quite sure what to expect.

A Time Long Past

The smell of the leather, the weight of the headdress, even the morning air took William Dietz back to memories of standing on a similar hillside as a young boy only eight years old. On that day many years ago, the sun too had not yet risen. His Uncle One Star had insisted they come to this place. What the boy did not know was this was to be his last day living on the reservation.

Dietz—or "Lone Star" as he was called—had been left behind on the Rosebud Reservation in South Dakota after his mother Julia "One Star" Dietz had died. Following her death, Dietz's father had left the reservation when the boy was only three years old. Dietz's Uncle One Star had agreed to teach the boy the ways of the Sioux and the Lakotas. The elder Dietz had promised that on this day, the boy's eighth birthday, he would return.

One Star had been pressing for the boy to look out toward the East, where the Lakotas believed visions of the future often lay. In his dreams, the young Lone Star spoke of seeing an eagle—the same vision One Star had for the boy on that very night. A vision was critically important to a young Sioux. It would divine which path his life was to travel, answering the critical question: would he be a hunter, a scout, or a warrior? In rare cases, the youth might be asked to be a medicine man. One Star knew the images would come when the time was right. The eagle was a powerful force. Many believed it to be a leader, but in truth, it was more of a guide. Images often depicted an eagle leading others through dangerous lands.

Not knowing what might lie ahead for his nephew, One Star could only watch and hope. But there would be no revelations this day. Only change. The only words he spoke to his younger charge as he led him off the hill were "Come now, little Lone Star. There is a big surprise waiting for you for your birthday."

Pullman

As the memories washed over Dietz, he opened his eyes to see the eyes of his players and their confused expressions. "The East reveals our future," said Dietz quietly, without acknowledging the players who had gathered around him. "If we did not succeed, it is because we do not trust the man next to us."

Now looking directly into the eyes of his players, Dietz revealed a message many of the players would remember for years. "The pain you feel, we all feel. The strength you bring is a strength we all share. Victory comes when you give all you have, knowing the man standing with you will do the same." Pausing, Dietz then finished, saying, "The burden now lies upon you."

With that, Dietz turned on his heels and walked away, leaving the team standing alone on the hillside. Doc Bohler stood, just as perplexed as the players. In his hands, he had a new list of player assignments, along with a new set of plays and formations. As the team wandered back to the practice field, Bohler passed the handwritten copies to his captains.

Few of the players spoke. The Oregon Aggies would be coming to town in less than one week.

Sunday Night

As Dietz wandered back into the gym that Sunday night, he was surprised to find Doc Bohler sitting at his desk, looking out his window. On the field outside, players were out getting in some late night practice.

What Coach Dietz didn't realize was that the players had never gone home.

No break for morning services. No breaks for lunch. Dietz may have underestimated the power of offering hope to a team that had endured more than its share of shame and embarrassment. Dietz himself hadn't escaped from the game unscathed. He would wander over to the hospital, with fears he had come down with a nasty case of pneumonia.

Night Practice

Coach Dietz gave the team Monday off as a reward for its hard work, but he wanted the players to return for a rare evening practice. That night, it was time to begin preparations for their first true game. Oregon would be coming to town on Saturday. Memories of the last meeting still lingered in many of the players' minds. Not just because of the close score, losing 7-0, but for the sheer brutality of the game that had left several players, including Captain Asa Clark, with serious injuries. But Coach Dietz had a surprise for the squad.

A large screen was on the wall, with a projector ready to go. It would be movie night for the team, something rarely done in 1915. But the featured attraction wasn't produced in Hollywood. It was shot entirely in Pullman the weekend before. Dietz had arranged for the alumni game to be filmed and the movie processed in time for tonight's practice.

It is one thing to imagine how your team looks from the stands, but quite another to see the game being played out before your eyes. The opening series looked promising until Bangs' fumble. Yet there was real chaos in the way the game played out. On paper, strategies seem easy. On film, the evidence was much different.

With the breaks between plays removed, the entire game could be witnessed in under half an hour. There wasn't much discussion. Yet Coach Dietz remained optimistic. What many saw in the film as failure, Dietz saw as promise. With a second, then a third replay, Dietz made sure he pointed out what was working and how to improve moving forward.

With each passing play, Coach Dietz tried to paint a picture in his players' minds—an image of how his team just might compete.

CHAPTER 2

OREGON

OREGON

Pullman, Washington
October 9, 1915

The Oregon football team had a number of good reasons to be confident. On paper, the game would be lopsided. All of the Oregon linemen weighed in over 190 pounds. Even moving the fullback Carl Dietz to the line would give State, at best, an average of 175 pounds. Oregon had sent a scout to the Washington State alumni game, and he returned to tell Coach Bezdek, "Washington State will not be a factor." In truth, the scout only watched a few early plays and then disappeared to a local restaurant to get out of the weather. But add in such factors as a new Washington State coach with an entirely new system and Oregon had plenty of reasons to be dismissive.

Oregon Coach Hugo Bezdek waved off any talk of the upcoming game, announcing he would be holding out several key players, going so far as to tell an Oregon paper, "I will not use my Captain and star quarterback Cornell in the game, unless needed in a pinch."

As the Oregon team rolled into Pullman the day before the game, it brought with it a brackish bullying attitude that started with its coach and filtered its way down. Coach Bezdek fully promoted an ugly image of his team. Born in Prague, Czechoslovakia and immigrating to the United States as a child, he had played fullback at the University of Chicago. Since his arrival, his team had developed a loud and obnoxious reputation with a love for playing dirty. As he ran his team through its first afternoon workout, Bezdek launched a series of taunts heard all across the Pullman campus. "I can't hear you boys!" Bezdek bellowed. "You need to holler out on every play or else the hogs might get us!" Urged on by their coach, his players continued to laugh and join in the fun.

Nearby Washington State coaches didn't need to say a word. Bezdek had just handed their Washington State players all the motivation they would need.

Rally

On the Friday night before the first game of the season, the Washington State student body threw a rally for the team, complete with what promoters called "a red fire" that used special powders to turn the bonfire flames bright red. Unfortunately, the notion of tossing flammable powder into the fire did not set well with several sorority house mothers who refused to allow their women to attend. Despite the damper, the rally worked to help charge up the fans and, to some extent, the team.

Coach Dietz stood before the crowd, his team lined up behind him, all dressed in their best game day suits. Stepping forward, Dietz pressured his fans, "I do not predict victory or defeat. The team has been working hard, and I believe they have a good chance to win…if you students give us the right kind of support. Are you with us?" In response, the crowd of several hundred young men cried out their allegiance.

As the roar died down, someone yelled out to the team captain, "Hey, Clark, how about it?"

Clark stepped forward to speak for the team, "Well, Oregon has a fast and heavy team. But we have an entirely new system that looks pretty good to me. I put the odds at being fairly even." It was a comment that left many in the crowd nodding in approval. After all, these fans would be happy watching a team that would just be able to compete.

Kick-Off

It was perfect weather for a Pullman afternoon in October. The skies were cloudy, with temperatures around the mid-70s. Oregon, having won the toss elected to receive. Looking back into the stands, Dietz saw a crowd of some 1,200 fans gathered, mostly students to witness today's contest. It was a good-sized crowd, but one that looked rather sparse sitting in stands designed to hold nearly 3,000. Dietz allowed himself one moment to capture it all. He was about to stand tall as a head football coach for a respectable college team. The moment was broken only by the roar of the crowd as Washington State's Carl Dietz kicked the ball high into the air, sending it the entire length of the field. The Oregon receiver had barely caught the ball before the young WSC freshman Ronald Fishback was in his face. With nowhere for the runner to go, Oregon would begin the game on its own 9-yard line.

Eager to get into the game, the defensive unit from Washington State raced onto the field, joining those already on the kicking squad. While most coaches used special teams to train up their new players, Dietz believed in putting his best players on the field for every play. The large linemen for Oregon rumbled up to the ball, smiling as if they were all in on some big secret. Behind the center stood Oregon's young replacement quarterback, Orville Montieth, in place of the team's star player, Captain Anson Cornell. The ball snapped and the Oregon line rose to push forward with a direct run toward the middle, its two large backs pressing forward to make a path for the speedy running back. With lightning quickness, the WSC line shot into the gaps, or dove at the legs of the offense, creating a large pileup of bodies that made it nearly impossible to run. Into this log-jam, the running back tried to maneuver, only to be stopped cold.

As quickly as the play ended, the WSC team was back on its feet and ready to go, a move that somewhat surprised the Oregon team, used to being able to meander back to the huddle and plot its next maneuver.

On the second play, WSC's defense suddenly became alive. Players were constantly shifting around, from side to side and from being down in a stance to standing straight up. In the confusion, the linemen for Oregon shot glances back and forth. How were they supposed to block someone who wouldn't hold still? At the snap of the ball, the WSC defense blasted into the offense with surprising speed. Rapidly exploiting this confusion, both Fishback and two other linebackers sprinted into the backfield to greet a surprised running back who could only put down his head and try to minimize the loss. Oregon had barely stood up from the play when WSC was back in position and ready to go. A confused Montieth looked over at his coach for instruction. The two had gone over a set list of plays they were to run, but no one had planned out that they would find themselves on third down with 14 yards to go and with their backs on the goal line at the beginning of the game. Coach Bezdek screamed back at his players, waving to his quarterback just to keep to the playbook. The next play called for a sweep to the side that would match his larger players out in the open field with the smaller State team. From the snap, Oregon expected to surge forward. Instead, the State team played match-up football and held the linemen in place. As the backfield sprinted out to the side, it was instantly met by the speedy players of WSC. First in line for Oregon was its large fullback who lowered his head to smash into the speeding Dick Hanley. But just as the fullback reached the point of impact, Hanley seemed to disappear, dropping to the ground and rolling into the fullback's legs. The momentum of the Oregon player sent him sprawling, while Hanley, in his well-practiced roll, popped up behind the blocker and sent the halfback into the ground with a quick tackle.

Just like that, Oregon had been stopped handily.

The speedy Washington State running back, Benton Bangs, raced into the game to receive the kick. Stepping back onto his 30-yard line, he grabbed the ball in mid-air, sprinting forward as quickly as possible. Across the field, a series of rolling blocks completely upset the timing of the Oregon defenders. With ease, Bangs moved the ball forward to mid-field. Coach Bezdek was beside himself. Racing onto the field, he screamed out at his players as they rose up to play defense. He paused in his rants long enough to see an entirely new team of players racing onto the field to play offense. Clearly, this Dietz had a few tricks up his sleeve. Coach Dietz was surprisingly calm, holding his quarterback close to go over strategy one more time.

All eyes were on the field to see what this new offense could deliver. Players were already set when the WSC quarterback Bull Durham raced to the field. "Apple-3," said Durham to the players as he passed behind them. A simple play, but one that best spoke to the development of this team from its very beginning. With the snap of the ball, the State offense operated as one. Large linemen, expecting to engage in a physical wrestling match, found linemen who dropped and attacked their legs. The ball snapped directly into the hands of the running back Bangs, which caused instant confusion as half the Oregon backfield followed quarterback Durham in the other direction. The eyes of the left side Oregon linebacker shot open when he realized a full gang of blockers was coming down on top of him. He never saw the lanky Washington State end, Dick Hanley, coming from his left to seal off the run.

When Bangs turned the corner, he saw nothing but empty field, which he would exploit for 40 yards before being dragged down from behind. Oregon's defenders had to get up quickly as they realized Washington State was already at the ball, ready for the next play. A quick snap and fullback Dietz came smashing into the line, untouched, to add another 10 yards. Washington State was now inside the Oregon 10-yard line. Two plays later, a substitution fullback, Basil Doane, was brought in as an extra backfield blocker.

The move was a deception to mask the truth that Doane himself would be getting the ball. Slamming into the line, Doane put down his head, and with a surprising feat of strength, the young fullback pushed hard enough to drive back three Oregon defenders until he found himself standing in the end zone.

Just like that, WSC was up 7-0.

The stadium erupted with fans who could not believe how easily their Washington State team had just marched the ball down the field and scored. Neither could Oregon coach Bezdek, who realized this Washington State team was legitimate. Walking over to his start quarterback, Anson Cornell, he told him, "Warm up. We might just need you after all."

Washington State kicked off again, with the same result. Only this time, the return man had expected the speedy tackler and was able to side-step the attack to bring the ball back to the 25-yard line. At the line of scrimmage, the State defense, well-rested after being on the sideline, was again moving all over the place. The stronger Oregon linemen, many of whom played both offense and defense, began to grow frustrated with the scheme. Three times, Oregon plunged into the line. Three times they came up with little to show for it. For the second time in a row, they would have to punt without having made a first down.

Washington State's Bangs would return the punt to the team's own 35-yard line. By arrangement, Quarterback Durham began to work the ball inside the tackles. First left, then right, each play earned at least 5 yards. What was taking its toll was that as soon as the play ended, State was nearly back to the line of scrimmage and ready to strike again. On fourth down inside the Oregon 35-yard line, Oregon finally made a stand, holding Washington State on four downs.

Washington State had set the tempo for a fast-played game. A tempo that clearly favored the hometown team.

Switching now to defense, Washington State's defenders hit the Oregon team even harder. From the very first snap, it appeared WSC was in the backfield, even before the ball could be handed off. For Oregon, it would be the very same story—three tries and then a punt. The game was moving along at a rapid pace. It was barely the second quarter when State took over from its own 25-yard line.

"Apple-4," Durham whispered to his players. But the play would not happen. On three, several Oregon players jumped off sides. Without a huddle, the defense was barely reset when State took off again with its sweep to the right. The Oregon players who had raced over to cover the play found themselves needing to sprint back to the line of scrimmage, barely in time for Washington State's Bangs running out to the left. Gaining 8 yards here, then 6 yards there, as frustrations began to mount on the Oregon side of the ball. Without warning, on the very next snap, the Oregon nose tackle, apparently tired of having Hack Applequist slamming his helmet into his chest, came up with a strong, right-handed fist that slammed into Hack's temple for a series of quick blows. Applequist, ignoring the assault, jumped up and was back over the top of the ball, ready for the next play. But Asa Clark noticed. Leaning back toward Durham, Clark asked for the inside Apple play—only Clark would not run behind the center. Instead, he pulled up and slammed his head directly into the offending Oregon lineman's face, giving him a bloody nose.

While a war was being waged along the trenches of the front line, the backfield continued to work its mastery. Soon, it was standing on the Oregon 20-yard line where Washington State had a secret play ready to go. By now, Oregon had been stretched out, running first to the left, then the right. "Bad Apple-3," Durham whispered to his players. The team lined up in its standard formation. Durham called out the count. On the snap, Applequist shot the ball into the hands of a running Bangs, who sprinted to the right. Blockers, as they had this entire series, raced to catch up. But instead of pushing forward with their rolling blocks, the players suddenly stopped.

Oregon, sensing a chance finally to catch the sprinting back for a loss, pressed hard to break through the wall. What it didn't notice was a missing fullback. Carl Dietz had run up to block at the line of scrimmage, only to slip out into the open area to the left side. With nowhere to run, Bangs suddenly stopped, lifted up the ball, and then tossed it far across the field to a wide-open Carl Dietz in the end zone.

Touchdown Washington State.

The crowd went crazy. Durham's kick was good and WSC now had a 14-0 lead with no sign of letting up. Even the newspaper writers in the press box had to be warned against cheering by the referee—something traditionally not allowed since journalists aren't supposed to show any favoritism.

Washington State's offense, rejuvenated by the moment, jumped up and down in excitement all the way to the sidelines. That is except for one player, Captain Asa Clark. While most eyes were on the ball, the Oregon line had set Clark up. The Oregon nose tackle had grabbed Clark's wrist and wrapped it under him as he fell to the ground. Two other linemen then slammed headlong into Clark as he was hunched over like a rabbit caught in a trap. As soon as the player struck, Clark could hear a tearing sound in his shoulder. The pain was immeasurable. Clark pulled his way free and headed over to the sidelines. He could not lift his right arm. With the celebration on the sidelines, no one noticed as Clark slipped to the bench and sat motionless.

On the Oregon sideline, Coach Bezdek remained frantic. Several of his top players, who hadn't even dressed for the game, were sent to the locker room for gear and were pressed into service. Pulling his star aside, Bezdek was seen screaming at his top player. The cocky quarterback, Cornell, brushed off the comment and strapped up his helmet to go to battle.

The move was not lost on Dietz, who pulled his defensive players aside as the ball was being kicked off. Dietz would switch his defensive scheme, dropping back four linebackers and three defensive backs. With the new quarterback in the game, Oregon would surely want to pass the ball. With the Washington State defense jumping around before the snap, Oregon tried to counter by going to a quick count.

"Hike!" yelled Cornell, turning with the ball in his hands to set up for a pass. Shooting into the gaps, the Washington State linebackers found several openings. Oregon's Cornell had hardly set up when he was suddenly scrambling for his life. Getting outside a tackler, he sprinted outside to the right, trying to outrun the speedy defense, but all that effort and energy was wasted since he barely made it back to the line of scrimmage. Cornell leapt to his feet, screaming at his players, "What the hell was that? Can't you stop a bunch of farm boys?"

The words were not lost on Washington State. From that point on, WSC defenders took to making animal noises just prior to the snap. Typically, a defense is not supposed to holler when a quarterback is snapping the ball, but the line judge may have heard the "farm boy" comment as well, for it was clear he would allow the taunts. On the next snap, State was ready. Two defensive linemen smashed together into the same spot between offensive linemen. But instead of pushing forward, they pushed the players to the side. Running into the gap from behind, the speedy Fishback hit the opening at full speed. Cornell hadn't even stopped to look for his receivers when he was slammed by the speedy linebacker. Both men crashed hard into the ground.

Washington State's Ronald Fishback jumped quickly to his feet and offered his hand to help Cornell up. The Oregon quarterback reluctantly agreed, but as he stood, Fishback pulled him close, saying only "Moo."

Not wanting to risk turning the ball over, Oregon decided to run for a first down, but it was again stopped short. The half was rapidly approaching, and not only had Oregon not had the ball past midfield, but it had yet to make a single first down. Playing it safe, Oregon would punt.

Doc Bohler glanced back to see a rather quiet Clark sitting by himself on the bench. As the ball was being punted, he walked over and said, "Hey, Clark, you O.K.?" Clark only nodded and strapped on his helmet with the only good arm he had left.

State now had the ball on its own 35-yard line. Running to the line of scrimmage, Clark moved the younger lineman Finney from his left guard spot over to tackle. Washington State quarterback Bull Durham had been told to keep the ball on the ground. There was still plenty of time left in the game. Noticing the change in the line, Durham just assumed it was something Coach Dietz had ordered. On the first play, fullback Carl Dietz grabbed the ball and headed over the right tackle. But as soon as the ball was snapped, Clark launched straight out at the Oregon nose tackle, delivering a solid left-handed fist to the temple. As the players fell into the pile, Clark didn't let up. Three, then four times, he slammed his hand into the nose tackle's head. Hidden under the pile, the referee didn't see what was happening. While Clark didn't have the leverage needed to strike a knockout blow, the message was clear: "Paybacks are coming."

The next play was to the right, but Clark shot straight out for one of the linebackers who had slammed into his shoulder. As Clark lowered his head to block, his left hand came crashing hard up into the linebacker's ribcage. "Ooof," was the only sound as the player's breath quickly left his body. Clark felt a sharp sting in his right shoulder as the player's partner decided to land a return blow; Clark simply turned and virtually ran the man over, dropping him to the ground, with Clark's knees driving straight into his chest. For Clark, this was no longer about a game. This was a personal war.

Neither of the Oregon players got up quickly, but they had no choice; Washington State was driving again. The line judge, who didn't have a clear vision of the melee, noticed the wobbly players holding their chests and stomachs. The referee went to Clark and said, "O.K., let's take it easy in there. I'm watching you."

The series had stalled with Washington State punting from the 50-yard line.

On the ensuing drive, Oregon got a break. State had begun substituting a number of younger players, one of whom was standing on the wrong side of the field when the runner broke loose. Using speed to make up for the gaffe, Washington State chased the runner down from behind. It was the first time Oregon had been onto the Washington State side of the field all game, with the ball just inside the 40-yard line.

Coach Dietz didn't seem to get too excited. Instead, he waved the droopy-headed defender back onto the field and praised him for catching up to the speedy back. With the closing seconds of the half, Oregon tried two rushed passes that went incomplete, and then he ran the ball off the right side to give their kicker a straight-on shot. Oregon's kick from the 35-yard line was good, and both teams headed into the locker room with the score WSC 14, Oregon 3.

What wasn't lost on Dietz was how several of Oregon's biggest players immediately dropped to the ground where they stood, choosing to sit instead of heading to the locker-room. The pressing Washington State offense had worn them out.

As Dietz looked up into the stands, he realized there were more fans now than at the game's beginning. As he led his players into halftime, he knew Coach Bezdek may have been caught off-guard, but he would not make the same mistake again. Players joyously jumped and cried out like the game had been won.

At the back of the pack, Asa Clark walked slowly. Doc Bohler noticed how he was favoring his right arm. "When did you do that?" Bohler asked. Clark, in an attempt to be stoic, was trying to mask his pain. "Oh, it's fine; just a bit of a sprain." Doc then closed the ranks alongside his captain and lightly pressed up on his right elbow. The immediate wince on Clark's face told him everything he needed to know. He'd separated the shoulder. "Let's get inside; I'm going to take a look at it." Doc Bohler had earned his nickname because of the care and concern he showed his players. Once inside the locker room, Clark could hardly remove his shoulder pads without Doc's help. Doc pretended to be giving Clark an exam, but in truth, he knew the shoulder had been separated. "Yes, it looks like a slight separation, Clark. You're not going back in." Clark angrily replied, "The hell I'm not."

Dietz, who had caught the conversation, came over and reiterated Bohler's concerns. "Clark, I need you on this team for the entire season. It won't kill you to sit one half." Clark sat motionless. As his anger subsided, the pain in his shoulder began to become more intense. After a long pause, Clark finally nodded in agreement. At least he had gotten even for his injury.

Over in the Oregon locker room, Coach Bezdek had begun his angry rant the moment his team had arrived and he would continue nonstop until the referee stuck his head in to tell them it was time to go. Bezdek now had all of his best players into the lineup. Over in the Washington State locker room, Coach Dietz took an entirely different approach. Just as he had during the game, he continued to work on individual coaching sessions. Approaching a number of the younger players, Dietz told them to expect more playing time in the second half. While his defense was playing well, he knew Oregon would be coming at them full force in the second half. Stopping them early would be critical. Pacing now, Coach Dietz outlined their second half strategy. His only rallying words were to be ready. Pausing now, Dietz looked around the room. His players had not tasted such a victory before, and they were eager to get back onto the field. He didn't need to say another word.

90

Second Half

As the teams returned to the field, the players themselves took notice of the growing number of fans in the stands. Word had spread quickly across campus, and fans were eager to see the ending. Receiving the ball first, Washington State's running back, Benton Bangs, fielded the opening half kick-off and returned the ball to the 30-yard line where he quickly popped up ready to begin.

Dietz watched as Oregon's defense took to the field. The coach had now spread the defense out wide and brought more men up closer to the line of scrimmage. Recognizing the team would try to focus on the run, Dietz instructed his quarterback, Durham, to try a few passes to keep them off guard. At the first snap, Durham grabbed the ball and set up, quickly looking for a receiver. Zimmerman was having a tough time shaking his man loose. On the other side, Dick Hanley cut inside his man and waved for the ball. Durham tried to get in to him quick, but at the last instance, an Oregon linebacker reached out and tipped the ball to the ground.

Quickly back to position, Durham called out a running play to the left. The stacked up line was able to contain Bangs as he moved outside the tackle. On third down, Durham called Carl Dietz's number off the left side, where the absence of Clark was felt, but the fresh new guard opened enough of a hole for a good 6-yard run. It wasn't enough. Washington State would need to punt.

On the sidelines, Doc Bohler had noticed something he wanted to tell his defensive leaders. Bohler noticed that when an Oregon passing play was called, the large Oregon linemen would barely set their hands on the ground, knowing they would be standing straight up to pass block. Bohler told his linebackers that when they saw this move, the linebacker with the fewest linemen on his side would need to try and rush the quarterback, while the other would drop back to help cover a receiver.

After the Carl Dietz punt, Oregon had the ball on its 40-yard line.

True to the rotation, Washington State's defense came on eager to go. Most of the Oregon players stayed on the field, having played defense, and were now switching gears to offense. From the first snap, Oregon had switched up its tactics. Instead of its linemen shooting out to make a block, the line stood straight up and used its arm strength to keep the defenders tied up. The running back found a gap and sprinted 7 yards—Oregon's biggest gain of the day.

On the next play, the Washington State linebackers stayed in tight to slow down the run. Oregon Quarterback Cornell dropped back to pass, making an easy 7-yard completion. It was Oregon's very first, first-down. Fishback and Hanley both looked at each other, knowing they had messed up. With its own quick snap count, Oregon moved the ball around the end for another 6 yards, for a first down and a renewed sense of momentum.

As Oregon rumbled up to the ball, both of the Washington State linebackers saw the Oregon linemen gently placing their hands down for a pass play, just as Bohler had noted. Hanley took one step forward; then he saw that Fishback had the open lane and dropped back into coverage. Fishback, with a head start, found himself in the backfield, just as the quarterback, Cornell, released the ball. Over the top of Hanley's head, the receiver grabbed the pass and ran down to the Washington State 40-yard line.

While the play might have rattled another team, Washington State stayed relatively calm. Just a few plays into the half and already the Oregon team showed signs of slowing. A run off right tackle was only good for a couple of yards. Then back to the left side for a sweep that State was able to push out with its speed. On third down, Hanley decided to make a crucial call. Both linebackers would go after the quarterback. For added measure, Hanley had the defense backs take an extra step backwards. Sure enough, Oregon wanted to pass. But Hanley and Fishback both had a head of steam when they hit the line, so they were soon chasing Cornell around. The quarterback had no choice but to get rid of the ball.

So from the 35-yard line, Oregon went for a field goal that went wide right. Washington State's lead held at 14-3.

On the sideline, Dietz had only a few words of encouragement, greeting nearly every player personally as he came off the field. Back on offense, Washington State returned to its form from the first half. Using a series of fakes and diversions in the backfield, a quick dive into the line by Carl Dietz would gain 5 yards, and Benton Bangs went around the end for another 7. Almost as soon as the team had downed the ball, Washington State was back at the line with another play. Simple—yet devastating. State marched the entire length of the field to Oregon's 20-yard line. Seeing how tired his boys were becoming, Coach Bezdek quickly called a time out. On cue, his players sat down, panting from all the extra plays State was running.

Dietz smiled. He had another surprise in store for Oregon. Waving over his receiver, Dick Hanley, Dietz had signaled for a special play—one that had been called "the reverse." Clarence Zimmerman nearly busted out smiling. It was a secret play the team had only just added to the list a few days before.

As the referee blew his whistle, Washington State was already lined up. Quarterback Durham dropped down to line up to the right of the center, and on the snap, he disappeared to the left to become a blocker. The right tackle and the fullback joined him. The ball snapped high in the air, landing in Benton Bangs' hands as he raced to catch up to a mass of blockers who had effectively run against Oregon all day. Only this time without warning, Zimmerman, who had been blocking his man, turned around and grabbed the ball from Bangs, going in the opposite direction. Bangs lowered his head with a fake, appearing to be driving for extra yardage. Oregon had been working so hard to stop the sweep that it never even saw Zimmerman, who raced to the sidelines and ambled in, almost completely unnoticed for the touchdown.

Washington State was now up 21-3.

The stadium erupted in pandemonium. From the students to the faculty to the people from town, not a single person was sitting down. Everyone was jumping up and down, screaming at the top of his or her lungs. Everyone, that is, except the 200 Oregon fans in the end zone who had traveled there from Eugene. It seemed the only one who was not celebrating was Coach Dietz. As he had all game, the Washington State coach spent his time talking individually with players.

There comes a time in every game when the coach becomes all but certain of the outcome of a match, long before it has come to its conclusion. As the fourth quarter began, the exhausted Oregon players could barely muster up a minimal offense. Dietz began to substitute players heavily in the fourth, even allowing players who had never played any of the skill positions to try their hands at running the ball.

On third down and long for Oregon, Zimmerman, still excited from his touchdown run, convinced his defensive backs into trying the special trick passing play they had come up with—one that baited the opposing quarterback into thinking a receiver had been left wide open. The players just smiled. As Oregon's highly rated quarterback, Cornell, brought his team to the line, he watched the left defensive back take a step toward the line as if he were going to try to charge the quarterback. Smiling, he knew a pass play would fix that, but he had to get rid of the ball quickly. "Hike!" the Oregon quarterback called out and dropped back to pass. With the defender rushing in from the side, Cornell stood firm, taking a hit just as he released the ball. Smiling as he hit the ground, he knew his receiver would be running for a score, especially when he heard the gratifying sound of the crowd erupting in cheers. But that smile began to fade as he realized the cheers were from Washington State fans. The Oregon quarterback had never seen the lanky defensive end Zimmerman step back from the line, raising up his long arms to tip the pass into his hands. Ambling down the sidelines, virtually untouched, Zimmerman would add his second touchdown of the day to put Washington State up for good, 28-3.

The rest of the game was pretty much a blur, as both sides began playing out their reserves. As the final gun sounded, the two coaches met at midfield. "I gotta say, Dietz, your boys played a hell of a game," Oregon Coach Beznek offered while extending his hand to Dietz for a longer than expected handshake. Dietz graciously responded, "We had a good day."

In the locker room, Dietz wandered around from player to player, offering up his personal congratulations and spending a minute reliving a game highlight of which the player had been part. With a few words of encouragement, players couldn't help but respond by saying, "Not a bad day for a bunch of 'farm boys.'" The offense had worked extremely well. The difficult to master body-roll the team had struggled with in camp now proved to open large holes in the defensive lines, especially against larger, heavier players.

Dressed in their Sunday best, the players would walk across campus with a more meaningful step as the pride of Washington State.

But there would be little rest for the victors. Practice had been set for 5 p.m. on Monday. There would be just over a week of practice ahead before the team headed south for its second key test—a football match up in Corvallis.

CHAPTER 3

OREGON AGRICULTURAL COLLEGE

OREGON AGRICULTURAL COLLEGE

Pullman, Washington
October 16, 1915

A bye week served as the perfect prescription to help players recover from the bumps, bruises, and overall fatigue suffered in the Oregon victory. Asa Clark's separated shoulder showed signs of healing, Arthur Durham nursed sore ribs while Clarence Zimmerman kept quiet about the muscle separation burning in his chest. By football standards, the team had not suffered badly. The new week brought with it the usual routines for these college athletes. All around them conversations could be heard about the team's win over Oregon, yet with rare exception, the players enjoyed anonymity. Few fans even recognized who these football players were at Washington State.

To break up his own routine, Coach Dietz chose a different route across campus, making his way through the art building where budding artists were at work. Dietz paused at a doorway, caught up in the sights and smells of his other passion—art. Noting several seats open at the back of the room, Dietz decided to slip in and grab a seat at a drawing table. Like a kid sneaking into a cinema, Dietz kept his head down, but he found himself enraptured by the feel of charcoal in his hands, pulling him toward the empty canvas. Without effort, Dietz drew the figure of an American Indian, using a style he had developed entirely on his own as a student at Carlisle. The charcoal soon became the image of a young Sioux warrior, his arms at rest, holding a long peace pipe complete with an eagle feather, a symbol of leadership. He so loved this form of art because it made his own people more realistic and human—much different than images of the "battling warrior" that dominated the art scene.

Dietz was so caught up that he never felt the gaze of a surprised instructor, one Miss Orilla Miner, now standing behind him in fascination. Miss Miner was not the art instructor; she was, in fact, the school's photography teacher pressed into service when the art teacher left school unexpectedly. When she asked what Dietz was doing, he replied he was drawing a picture of his uncle, One Star. Miner found herself mesmerized by the artistic magic pouring onto the paper. When she asked him to share his art with the class, Dietz rose quickly, eager to share his passion. For the students only here a few weeks, the presence of a new face may not have surprised them. But many had to sit up in their seats when Dietz revealed the drawing he had made in such a short period of time.

Without prompting, Dietz began working his way around the room, reviewing each drawing, offering praise. His voice attracted the attention of Bruce McCully, the department head, who was passing through the hall. Meeting him at the doorway, Orilla Miner offered, "He just showed up in class and began to draw. But just look at him; he seems like a natural at this." McCully leaned toward Miss Miner and said, "You do realize that's our new football coach, William Dietz."

Orilla smiled, but she really did not understand what the chair was saying. McCully smiled as well. He would talk to the president, of course, but McCully was fairly certain he had just found his new art instructor.

Classwork

McCully was busy with a campaign of his own. He posted notices of a contest offering a $100 prize for the best essay on ending the war in a peaceful fashion. Entitled the "International Arbitration Contest," the prize was being offered up by one of the top professors at Harvard.

The Austrian-Serbian conflict had now spilled over into its neighboring territories. Russia had backed the Serbs, causing Germany to back the Austrians. When Germany asked France to take sides, leaders refused, so the Germans declared war on the French. Now the British, who were allied with Belgium, declared war on Germany. Would the United States be dragged into the conflict?

What bothered Bruce McCully the most was the building fervor for the war among college students. Several students had already left school to join the war on both sides. He spoke on the subject at length in his lectures, knowing this material might seem inappropriate for an advanced English class. Yet, McCully feared the romanticizing of battle that often touched the hearts of young men. An overseas adventure under the banner of a noble cause had long been a siren call to a young man eagerly searching for his own place in the world.

On campus, several federal speakers talked in support of the war overseas. John Mott, for example, had brought back firsthand accounts of the atrocities being committed against common folk. Many of these college students were themselves first or second generation immigrants with ties back to Europe. Even the local Baptist minister had begun raising lessons from the Bible in support of Americans taking up the battle in Europe. "The inevitable conflict" was among the more popular phrases.

It was this call to arms McCully feared the most. His literature books were filled with seductive calls, ending with countless lives lost for causes that, with the fullness of time, rarely seemed noble or, even more tragically, worthwhile.

Telegram

The win over Oregon had ignited a true excitement among the students. But in the era of no Internet or even radio, fans would often wait days to hear how their favorite teams had done.

William Nessly had an idea. What if someone could wire back dispatches to Pullman so fans could know how the game was progressing almost as soon as it happened? Nessly was somewhat of a local favorite, having grown up in Pullman. At the college, he had just started up the student newspaper *The Evergreen*, where he served as its first editor and reporter. After all, his father, J.E. Nessly, was a newspaper man of note who often traveled out of town to cover big stories for the regional newspapers. William Nessly would be following in his father's footsteps by traveling to Corvallis to cover the game.

But William needed a partner, and he found one in a visiting student from Scotland, Hector McBean Hart, who knew how to use a teletype keypad. Hart was Nessly's friend and partner at the student paper. The Pullman telegraph office was now operating the new "Stick Punch" machine that could send messages up to seventy words a minute. That is, when everything ran smoothly. Unfortunately, in this small town outpost, there were plenty of times when the system didn't work. William's mother, Cora Nessly, was proficient as well, having worked in the telegraph office for years. Her role would be to assist in receiving and transcribing the messages once they were sent.

If the two WSC students could pull this off, they would be making history.

Practice

With a light week off, it was time for the Washington State players to focus on the upcoming Saturday game. The team would be traveling to Corvallis, Oregon, to take on The Oregon Agricultural

College "Aggies." Coach Dietz knew this would be a difficult test. Also known as OAC, the team returned a number of starters who had been invited to play Michigan State in East Lansing, Michigan, in a few weeks. For years, sportswriters had called for the West to play the East. Michigan State was considered to be one of the Eastern teams, having built up a national reputation by beating some of the best the East had to offer.

If history held true, Washington State was in trouble. Six times, WSC had traveled to Corvallis. Six times, State had met defeat. Yet Coach Dietz spent most of the week with a focus on conditioning, while he worked to implement new schemes specially designed for OAC. The Washington State coach made it clear there would be no scrimmaging.

OAC

To say that the Oregon Agricultural College took the upcoming contest against Washington State College lightly would be an understatement. Instead, coaches were focused on the upcoming Michigan Aggies game. But the Oregon Agricultural College head coach, E. J. "Doc" Stewart, had other immediate problems. He relied on information from his advance scout to build a game plan for his team. Sitting across from him was the captain of last year's squad, Everett May, whose report had left him baffled.

May had been one of OAC's top players the season before. Hiding in the weeds near the stadium, Stewart had been assigned to write down everything he could about the Washington State game.

But what Everett had written didn't make any sense.

Coach Stewart looked closely at the diagram his assistant had drawn. The formation seemed wrong. One back was missing. It seemed like they had lineman running to both the left and right. The only thing that made sense was that the Washington State team liked to run the ball.

The rest of the report seemed stranger than fiction. Stewart couldn't describe how the defense was lined up, insisting that players were moving all the time.

But Stewart did offer some hope. Washington State didn't have anyone on the team over 185 pounds. His OAC boys would clearly out-class them by sheer size.

Preparation

Washington State Coach William Dietz smiled as he looked into the mirror. He hadn't worn this outfit since his high fashion days visiting the best art galleries of Pennsylvania and New York with his lovely bride. Starting at the top, Dietz wore the latest in beaver skin tall hats, with a matching black wool coat lined with silk and flared with tails. His custom-made gray pants with a black signature line down the side fit well. Completing the look were new shoes with a high glossy shine and a brass topped walking stick. Yes, this was the look he needed to establish himself as the leader of these men. Dietz, as always, wanted to make an impression.

Campus

"Pug" Barnes wasn't satisfied.

The cheer coach looked around the auditorium and realized that what was missing from this football rally was the football team. A glance at the clock gave him an idea. The train had not left. If they hurried, they might just make it.

Racing over to the marching band, Pug waved his arms wildly in front of the conductor until the music stopped. Standing on a chair, Pug called out, "Let's give our boys a proper sendoff!" Jumping down, he grabbed the drum major and led the band out the door. Along the way, Pug somehow picked up a megaphone and began leading new cheers as the fans weaved their way through campus. By the time the fans had reached the station, an initial crowd of 150 students had grown to well over 600. The train was still in the station, but the team members were already in their seats. Undeterred, Pug began to chant, "We want Coach. We want Coach." Soon, the crowd began to follow, unwilling to give in until the coach appeared. Out of the back door came Dietz, basking in the undulation being offered.

"What brings you out on such a day as this?" Dietz asked the crowd, which only elicited an even louder response.

As the cheers faded, Dietz continued saying, "On behalf of the men of this fine Washington State football team, I want to thank you for your tremendous support. Against the boys from Oregon—it was as if you were right there helping us push into the line—and with your support..." Dietz paused for effect, "these boys don't stand a chance."

An enormous cheer rose up as fans felt like the coach had just given them credit for the win. One by one, the players began filtering out on the platform at the back of the train car.

"How bad are you going to beat O-A-C?" came a call from the crowd.

"Now, now," Dietz answered, his hands waving in a calming fashion, "thanks to this wonderful sendoff, I can guarantee these men will give those Corvallis eleven all the fight they can handle right to the very last."

Undeterred, the crowd wanted a clear declaration of victory. Calling out to the captain, one fan yelled, "Hey, Clark, how about you? Can you promise a win?" The normally quiet Clark would only say, "I stand by what the coach says; we'll give them a fight they're not expecting!"

With the sound of the departing train's steam whistle, the marching band led fans into a rather raucous song to send the team off. Inside the train, the players made their way back to their seats; many must have smiled to themselves at all this newfound attention.

Game Day

A hot Corvallis afternoon gave way to a muggy evening, as the Washington State players took to the field wearing their traditional wool pants and leather helmets. Whatever discomfort they felt quickly dissipated. Players seemed lighthearted, even impatient, for the game to begin. WSC Coach Dietz's outward confidence hid any concern he may have felt with the sheer size and number of players on the Oregon Agricultural College side of the field. While few homes in the Northwest had modern electrical conveniences, the football field at the Oregon Agricultural College had large lights that surrounded the field on tall poles.

Tensions had been broken the evening before as a heckler in the stands tried his utter best to shake the players up during a practice session. An endless stream of taunts, insults, and even profanities didn't stop until Washington State Assistant Coach Tyrer took it upon himself to talk with the young man. Tyrer could be an imposing force when needed. The team was surprised to see Tyrer, with the heckler in tow, appear before them. This boisterous fan, moments before filled with bravado, now stood embarrassed and sheepish. "Men, this is Billy," said the grinning Tyrer. "Billy here is a Washington State fan—and thought you were Oregon." The entire team laughed in unison. By the time Billy left, he'd shaken the hands of nearly everyone on the team, pledging to be a "one-man cheering machine" the next night.

Dietz now walked the sidelines in the same outfit he had donned for the trip. A dashing figure, he was filled with the confidence of a field general marching his troops into battle. The journey wasn't easy. Every day was a challenge to instill these new facets of the game— ideas that had taken years for him to develop. A handful of sports writers didn't know what to make of this new figure. Few gave this new coach and his team a chance.

Dietz whispered something to his game's co-captain, Hack Applequist, who broke out into a smile before heading out for the coin toss. "Tails," said the referee. "Washington State, do you want the ball first?" Smiling, Applequist remembered the swagger displayed by Oregon the week before. "No, we'll defend the east goal." Washington State was refusing to take the ball first.

Pausing momentarily, the players from OAC added back their own sense of gamesmanship. "We'll take the ball in the second half," they said, meaning that despite their attempt, Washington State would get the ball first.

Kick-Off

A high, booming kick dropped into the hands of Washington State's Basil Doane, who raced up the sidelines for a quick 20-yard return to the OAC 40-yard line. Against Oregon, Doane had proven to be a powerhouse at fullback. On the first play, Alfred Langdon surprised everyone with a bad snap that nearly shot over quarterback Bull Durham's head. Acting quickly, the Washington State quarterback grabbed the ball out of the air to prevent a turnover. Running forward, he reached the line without a gain, but without a loss. On second down, the team tried another run up the middle, with no gain. On third down, Washington State tried running around the end, but it was stopped at the line of scrimmage. The only bright spot from this series, WSC's Carl Dietz would blast a booming punt that pinned Oregon back to its own 15-yard line.

It was now the Washington State defense's turn to hold back OAC. From the very start, the Aggies' offensive line appeared confused as the State players jumped around, right up until the very snap; then suddenly, they seemed to come out of nowhere to swarm the ball carrier. Three plays later, Oregon would now be forced to punt.

Pullman

The grand telegram experiment was in full swing. Sitting in

the press box, the two WSC newspapermen were busy sending back dispatches as promised. Cora Nessly had her hands full transcribing the words while trying to follow the action. Her Washington State boys were fighting tough down in Corvallis.

A voice from behind her said, "Cora, I'm glad you're still open." It was a local farmer. A quick raised left hand told him he'd need to wait as she continued to write out the message with her right hand. Confused, the local man stood quietly in hopes he could get a late night message off before she closed for the weekend.

Corvallis

On their next drive, Washington State Quarterback Bull Durham put together a masterful game plan to work the ball down the field. On third down now from the OAC 25-yard line, he called out the trick play that had worked so well the week before. The ball snapped right into the hands of the speedy Benton Bangs, who ran to the right, pulled up to stop, and suddenly threw the ball to the left. Durham had slipped past the defender and was wide open. At the last second, one of the large linemen for Oregon raised up his tall arms and barely tipped the ball out of reach, saving a touchdown.

As Durham headed back to the huddle, he whispered to his team "Pass on three," meaning the team would quickly drop back into a passing formation. As the ball was snapped, Durham raced back as if to pass, but then he deftly released the ball for a drop kick. Just as it touched the turf, his strong foot came through, driving the ball into the air and over the crossbar.

Washington State now led 3-0.

Pullman

"Yes!" Cora said aloud as she deciphered the final letters. For too many years, she had seen her boys fall to the mighty teams from

Oregon. While the game was still early, her Washington State boys were on the scoreboard first.

Glancing up, Cora saw her customer's confused look. Embarrassed, she revealed her secret.

"I'm sorry; it's just that State just scored first on Oregon, so I got a little excited."

Even more confused, the local man looked on, hoping for an answer. Cora wanted to explain, but she rushed back to her chair as another set of dispatches was coming.

Corvallis

The two teams continued to battle in a tight game. With the ball, Washington State would use its speed to try and outrun the stronger OAC team, but the athleticism of the boys from Corvallis found a way to make a shoestring tackle or just get a hand on a jersey to make the stop. On the Washington State sidelines, Coach Dietz still showed little concern as he focused instead on individually coaching select players as they came off the field.

WSC Captain Asa Clark came off the field with a more excited attitude. Already, his players had held their ground with these highly-skilled and oversized beasts from OAC. Yet Clark began to see cracks developing in their armor. The relentless offense already had many of their defenders panting for air. Clark didn't have long to wait. A high 50-yard floating kick by Carl Dietz had Oregon's Lee Bisset backed up to his own 10-yard line. All day long, the speedy Ron Fishback had been the first to race down the field, almost seemingly untouched, with Clarence Zimmerman right behind him. The approaching duo caught the attention of OAC's receiver Bisset, who looked away at the wrong time and promptly dropped the ball to the ground. Fishback, shoulders lowered for the tackle, pushed him out of the way. Right behind, Zimmerman promptly dropped onto the ball, popping right back up, eager to get the next play going.

Washington State would take over on the Oregon Agricultural College 8-yard line.

With a rush, the Washington State offense raced onto the field. Quarterback Durham quickly called the play, "Apple-2." The ball snapped right into the hands of running back Benton Bangs, who raced to the edge only to be stopped after just a 2-yard gain. Without pause, Washington State lined up for an inside blast. In a repeat of what had happened the week before, Durham faked to Carl Dietz, who raced to the outside, then slipped the ball into the hands of the hard-headed Doane, who pushed behind Ace Clark for the touchdown, just as the gun went off, signaling the first half had concluded.

Washington State would end the first half with a 10-0 lead.

Pullman

A loud cheer erupted from inside the Western Union Telegraph Office. A steady stream of interested onlookers had gathered to hear the latest updates from Corvallis. Not only was it a novelty to hear the results of the game happening hundreds of miles away, but the idea that State might actually be ahead of OAC sent a ripple through this small town. The only challenge was for Cora to keep from cheering herself before she had the chance to read the dispatch out loud to the others. Keeping her composure, she read the latest dispatch:

"Oregon fumbles their punt. State scores. 10-0 at the half."

"Can I take this?" asked a smiling young student from the college. The young freshman had been told in advance that these messages had a chance of working, and he was eager to spread the news.

There was a big dance that night on the Washington State campus, so this news couldn't wait. Bursting into the hall, out of breath, the freshman was met by a curious "Pug" Barnes. Pug glanced down at the Western Union stationary. His face lit up in excitement as he read the brief dispatch. Standing on a nearby chair, Pug read the telegram to the gathered students. At first, there was confusion that someone would have the actual results of the game while it was still going on. But recognition soon replaced disbelief as the crowd began dancing its way around the hall in celebration.

Pug eagerly convinced the boy to keep running dispatches back to the dance. On the wall, Pug enlisted help in handing up streamers to create a small football field—something to help these fans visualize the game being played out in Corvallis.

Corvallis

The OAC players' long faces from the game's first half had vanished and been replaced by a renewed team charged up for the second half—a big change from how they had appeared just before halftime when a number of Oregon players, especially among the larger linemen, had dropped to their knees to sit and rest.

Coach Dietz took note and called for his team to begin quickly. Fatigue would again be his team's greatest ally. Racing onto the field, many of the players were smiling as if in on a private joke. Just two games into the season and these Washington State men had begun to take on a true swagger, bestowing the confidence needed to be true champions.

Yet from the kick-off, it was clear OAC still had plenty of fight. The home team started the half with the ball on its own 25-yard line. The Washington State defense, fresh from playing a speedy game, seemed even more active than before. Lining up outside the tackles, Washington State's plan worked to press Oregon into itself. OAC tried to move en masse, but time after time, State's plot to pile them into each other kept working. Once again, the Oregon Aggies would fail to make a first down and needed to punt.

On the sidelines, quarterback Bull Durham and Coach Dietz spoke briefly. The Washington State teammates had become pretty good at remembering a few plays in a row. Working to keep the ball in the middle, Washington State went to work. Bangs tried to head up the middle for no gain. Durham sprinted to the right behind a wall of men for 4 yards. A relative newcomer to the backfield, Ralph Boone came in with fresh legs and delivered another 4 yards inside the tackle and then 2 more off the right for a first down. The freshman was so excited to play he was already lined up in the backfield, ready to go, before the ball could even be set by the referee. With an almost workman-like quality, Washington State ground the ball down the field. No play ever netted more than a few yards, but each would be enough to keep the drive moving. OAC finally held inside its own 20-yard line, so on fourth down, Quarterback Durham grabbed the snap, stepped back, and dropped another beautiful kick over the crossbar.

Washington State was now in front 13-0.

Pullman

The crowd at the Pacific Bell Telegraph office now spilled out onto the street as hundreds gave a mighty cheer following each announcement. Farmers, businessmen, and students all joined together like they were all old friends. The game bound them together with a sense of unity as if each shared a collective secret. Their hometown boys being on top made the moment glorious.

A steady stream of freshmen now took up the job of running each dispatch to the growing crowd at the dance. With each telegram, a paper football was moved back and forth with fans cheering as if they were on the sidelines themselves. Pug Barnes was a continual source of energy. With his megaphone in hand, he raced around the gym, leading a series of cheers and song.

Gridiron Battle

As the Washington State defense gathered around Dietz, the players were all fresh and ready to go. The third quarter was nearly over, yet they had only played for a few downs. Tommy Tyrer had been sent down to watch the OAC team before and knew they would often resort to a secret play of their own late in the game—a "double-pass," as it was called, similar to what the Washington State team would offer. The difference being that their quarterback would toss the ball to his running back, then sneak out in the other direction to become a receiver.

Sensing the play would be coming, the team was ready.

As the defense raced out, Dietz looked back to see Doc Bohler tending to his utility man, Hack Applequist, who clutched his chest in serious pain. "How are you doing, Mr. Applequist?" Dietz asked as he walked up and put a hand on his shoulder. "A little rough, sir," said Applequist, who not only grimaced in pain but appeared to be having difficulty breathing.

Turning now to Doc, Dietz said under his breath, "Why don't we get the Oregon doctor here to take a look." Dietz was concerned Applequist may have suffered broken ribs, maybe more.

With OAC facing third down, the team tossed the ball to its sprinting running back who, just as Tyrer predicted, ran out to the right to avoid the Washington State rush. Then without warning, the back planted his foot and unleashed a long pass to the other side as the OAC quarterback headed to the open area. But Washington State's Ronald Fishback knew what was coming and delivered a powerful block to the quarterback before the ball was in the air, leaving it to drop onto the grass with virtually no one near. The Aggies would be punting.

Washington State's offense couldn't wait to get back out. Fresh and rested, they knew the OAC players had been on the field for the entire game. With Applequist out, fullback Carl Dietz dropped down to play lineman. In a relentless charge, the rested WSC offense jumped up as soon as each play finished, launching repeatedly into the exhausted defense. Only the whistle of the referee could save the day for OAC as the quarter came to an end. On the sidelines, Dietz began substituting in new players. He knew the only way to keep this push going was with fresh legs on the ground. It was almost like workers trying to move an enormous rock; once you started to feel it moving, you only need one last push to break it free.

With the start of the fourth quarter, Washington State began its punishing style just inside Oregon territory. Bangs hit the line for 3 yards; then Freshman Boone hit it for four more. The OAC coach frantically tried coaxing his players up off the ground and back into the fray, but Washington State just kept coming. The Aggies even tried their own hand at getting substitutions into the game, but they weren't fast enough. A costly penalty on the OAC defense for having too many men on the field pushed the ball down to the Oregon 11-yard line.

Washington State was about to strike a knockout blow.

In the huddle now, as the referees paced off the penalty, Durham gave his team three plays in a row to run. First would be Benton Bangs over the left tackle for 3-yards, but he was stopped. Boone tried the same spot, but only gained two. Durham tried the same spot, but was stopped cold. An Oregon injury gave both sides a quick breather. In the huddle, Durham made the call on fourth down to go for it. It would be a reverse to Hanley. The ball was snapped directly to Bangs, who shot off to the right in what appeared to be another of Washington State's big sweeps until Bangs slipped the ball to Dick Hanley racing the other way from the end. Looking for a spot, he saw the end zone open up just past the big tackle. Cutting sharply, Hanley's foot caught a loose piece of grass sod, tripping him up just short of the goal line.

Out of habit, the Washington State offense jumped back up to the line of scrimmage, several players not realizing they had just turned the ball over. Looking at the referee, Durham saw him raise his hands, indicating it was still fourth down. In reality, it was a fifth down. In the confusion, Freshman Boone raced off the field. Hanley jumped into his spot in the backfield as the ball was snapped into his hands. Racing around the corner, Oregon didn't stand a chance. Touchdown—for Washington State, in what would forever be remembered as the "five play drive."

The score was 20-0, with WSC in the lead.

Pullman

Cora Nessly jumped at the loud cheer that echoed as she read off the score. A fight nearly broke out among the freshman runners, eager to race this latest dispatch up the hill, with the group deciding they would all run up in unison to deliver the news.

Corvallis

After holding Oregon once again, Dietz began to substitute as many players as possible. But the relentless style of play led Washington State inside the OAC 30-yard line, close enough for another Bull Durham dropkick.

Washington State led 23-0.

On offense, Oregon came out passing, this time with better success. With Fishback on the sidelines, the quarterback had more time to throw. A 10-yard completion here, an 8-yard pass there, and soon Oregon was well inside Washington State territory. Play stopped when WSC was hit with a costly holding penalty of 15 yards.

Doc Bohler knew what Oregon would do. But would its trick defensive play work two games in a row? Smiling, Bohler called out "The Zimmerman."

Just as he did against Oregon, Zimmerman crowded the line as if

115

to rush the quarterback, while the WSC cornerback moved right up next to him, leaving the wide receiver open for the short pass. Zimmerman watched the OAC quarterback's eyes glance over with the move. Smiling to himself, Zimmerman had seen this before. On the snap, the receiver raced toward the open area. Just as the quarterback released the ball, Zimmerman stepped back into a now familiar pose—with the ball deflecting into his outstretched hands. Rumbling down the sidelines, Zimmerman would go 70 yards untouched, giving Washington State its final score of the day. Bull Durham was laughing so hard at the audacity of it all that he couldn't quite get the extra point to fall. While the clock showed several minutes left, this game was essentially over.

Washington State 29—Oregon Agricultural College 0.

Coach Dietz couldn't stop smiling. While reporters tried to give credit to his new style of play, Dietz insisted the credit all belonged to his players.

Returning Victors

The impact of their victory didn't hit the WSC team until the train arrived in Pullman early Monday morning. Hack Applequist had remained behind in the hospital with fears he had suffered a bruised liver and a broken set of ribs. The good news was he had only suffered some torn cartilage in his ribcage and would be following the team home soon. Although not a life-threatening injury, it was likely one that might cost him the rest of the season.

Benton Bangs, on the other hand, looked like he had been on the losing end of a bad fight. His face was left puffy and darkened from repeatedly lowering his head into the line as he fought for every yard. Many voted him their favorite player of the game. Most of the players were busy reading textbooks or writing as much as the rolling train would allow. After all, these were students as well as athletes. The team did not have a game this week, giving the players time to catch up on their schoolwork. Next up would be

WSC's annual rivalry game against the University of Idaho.

As the train rolled into the Pullman station, players were startled by a large cheer. Some 500 fans had gathered to welcome home the returning champions. At the front was rooter king Pug Barnes, who stood waiting at the ramp for the team to arrive. The players stepped sheepishly from the train as the crowd roared again. A giant banner had been painted saying "Our Champions." Whistles and bells rang out all across the city. Pug Barnes quieted the crowd and pulled out a rolled proclamation, read in his best Shakespearean style. "Citizens of this great land," Pub began, "we welcome back into our folds the great Washington State giants of the gridiron!" to which another enormous cheer erupted in the crowd. Pug continued, "Having vanquished their foes from Oregon, they now return into the bosom of their homeland to prepare for the great rivalry against the rapscallions of Idaho." A few boos came out, but mostly fans were laughing at the bawdy reference.

Pug continued, "Before our conquerors take to that field of battle, let us celebrate this great victory with a special dance Friday at Peppy Chapel to be held in their honor. Sincerely, your most humble fans."

The throng of fans then pushed the players toward a series of carts. Long ropes tied to the carts were taken up by fans eager to pull their champions up the hill to campus. A look of confusion spread across most of the players' faces. At first, they were surprised by the number of people here to greet them. But there was something else. There were a number of young women in the crowd who now appeared to be quite interested in them.

Reaction

Powerful back-to-back wins over Oregon and the Oregon Agricultural College could not be ignored by the Western Washington media since each defeated team had been the dominant favorite in its region. But WSC's acknowledgment still carried a veiled derogatory defamation of the institution, saying, "It was a wild night at Pullman last Saturday night when the news reached there that Washington State College had walloped OAC at Corvallis 29-0. The farmers stood around and yipped and yelled until their thoraxes were sore. Some of the boys have powerful lungs from calling hogs for the twilight meal."

Harsh words for a college struggling desperately for respect.

But the season was still young.

Pi Beta Phi

Sororities were a relatively new feature on many college campuses. The Pi Beta Phi chapter—its members were nicknamed Pi-Phis— was among the oldest and most prestigious on the Washington State campus. The symbol of the Pi-Phis was an arrow, which many of the girls joked was from Cupid himself.

Yet a few girls found themselves in a bit of a quandary. While they had agreed to help host the dance for the returning football team, more than one girl had expressed an interest in the very same man: one Captain Asa Clark. All of which was ironic since Clark, an older student at the age of twenty-eight, rarely went out with anyone on campus.

Among Clark's female fans were two young women who had made their intentions clear to the rest of the house—Lillian McDonald and her close friend Helen Quarrels. Each was a distinct contrast to the other. Lillian was rather quiet and reserved, studying to be a schoolteacher. Helen, a year younger, captivated many a young suitor with her light figure, straight brown hair, and light blue eyes. Unlike her friend, Lillian had dark curly hair, which she often wore up because of its unruliness. Her body was considered shapely. While Lillian was a strong athlete, Helen was more of a gentle spirit. They remained close friends. But as the dance came closer, they both found themselves having set their sights on the same man.

Pasadena

For twenty-five years, the City of Pasadena searched for national standing. Its annual Tournament of Roses festival remained popular among the locals, a tradition patterned after the "Carnaval des Fleurs" (Carnival of Flowers) in Nice, France. But leaders struggled for the right formula that would indelibly lead them to become "first in festival activities—both parade and sports." For years, the festival had tried a variety of events ranging from chariot racing to Olympic style individual sports. What bothered many was the somewhat "circus-like" atmosphere that had begun to creep in. A race between an elephant and a camel ended poorly when the elephant stopped short of the finish line, refusing to budge. Ostrich races provided more comedy than competition. In the last race, a rider was thrown from his mount right in front of the judging stand, and he was kicked across the ring when he tried to climb back aboard.

Yet the pageantry of the Tournament of Roses Parade had become truly spectacular. Horse-drawn floats were rapidly disappearing to be replaced by motorized vehicles. Large cities like Portland and San Diego now sent entries to promote their towns. Thousands of flowers were hand-tied to each float by tireless volunteers. With an upcoming change of leadership, many believed it was time to find a sporting event as grand as the annual parade.

Dr. Francis Rowland had been there from the very beginning. "We'd better go back to football," he advised. Not a popular position. Back in 1902, the tournament had tried to host its first football game. The idea was to bring in a national team to face a local favorite. In this case, Michigan matched up with Stanford. But, in truth, the game wasn't much of a contest. Michigan would win handily 49-0, a thrashing that didn't leave much of an appetite for football among the locals.

But the new leaders saw things differently. The football game had made a small fortune—$4,800 dollars to be exact, enough to purchase the land where the polo grounds now stood. With football gaining in national popularity once again, incoming Tournament of Roses President Lewis Turner wanted to revisit the idea, but only on the premise that the committee "lands the biggest championship football game" that could be scheduled. "So that Pasadena can give newspapermen from coast to coast something exciting to write about," Turner said.

Heading up the committee would be A.J. Bertonneau, a tall, dapper man who preferred to wear the long, full moustache made popular in Britain, but not yet popular in the States. Bertonneau had risen to the top of the Pasadena Board of Trade by making trades and investments that always seemed to turn to gold. His latest venture, a community-wide telephone system for Pasadena, had been among the first in the country. Meanwhile, construction crews were busy making good on his play to pave the roadways in order to sustain connectivity to his fair town.

But one key question filled his mind: could a football game put Pasadena on the national map?

The Dance of Champions

The week leading up to the big dance had been a strange one for the Washington State football players. Girls who never gave them the time of day before were suddenly making eye contact and saying, "Hello" as they passed. Students, strangers the week before, came up to ask casually about the game. Professors, normally aloof and distant, were suddenly friendly and engaged. There was even a rumor that one of the profs had offered to "share" his cough medicine with the players; medicine that was in fact good ol' fashioned corn whiskey—something a bit scandalous during these prohibition days of Pullman.

Coach Dietz had finally arrived by mid-week, telling tales of entertaining the aristocracy of Portland. He kept practice to a minimum, focusing instead on conditioning and running, always running. Hack Applequist was back on campus less upset with his injuries than what happened after the team had left. When he was released from the hospital, a local fraternity took him in for the night. Two waitresses from the nearby Corvallis Hotel pooled their tips to buy him flowers. Unfortunately, when they arrived at the house, the student answering the door insisted Hack had died. Stricken with grief, they sat down crying until a passing student told them the truth. Angered at the ugly tale, the pair threw down the flowers and stormed off. Hack wouldn't learn of the event until he was boarding the train for home.

The team had decided to travel over to the dance en masse. Arriving fashionably late, the team walked through the double doors of the dance without moving more than a few feet inside. As their eyes adjusted to the room, it was clear a lot of work had gone into the decorations. Music was playing fairly loudly as all eyes seemed to focus in their direction. Pug Barnes was the first to break the ice. "Gentlemen, welcome to the night of champions."

As the men gradually fanned out, several ladies approached with pads and pencils in hand for the time-honored tradition of asking them to add their names to their dance cards. Asa Clark was startled when two, then three, then four ladies all appeared before him, presenting their cards for his signature. All smiled pleasantly enough, but you could see the harsh glances they sent each other as they jostled for position. Appearing on his side was the team's running back, Benton Bangs. The two men could not have looked more different. Bangs, a thin but athletic man, looked younger than most because of his blonde hair combed down each side, leaving a straight part up the middle. Clark, despite dark hair that had begun its recession backwards, was a somewhat imposing figure with a man's well-developed body.

Lillian was the first to speak up. "Mr. Clark, just go ahead and make any mark you like here. I have taken the liberty of filling my dance card with your name, and your name only." Realizing she had been out-maneuvered, Helen quickly presented her card to the younger man, saying "Mr. Bangs, I have so enjoyed watching you play. Please do me the courtesy of being my partner this fine evening."

Neither man had much experience in this area. Glancing at each other, they shrugged their shoulders, took the pencils they had been handed, and did what these ladies had asked, not realizing the gamesmanship that had just taken place.

CHAPTER 4
IDAHO

IDAHO

Moscow, Idaho
October 30, 1915

A natural rivalry forms when two land-grant colleges are situated only eight miles apart. A state line was all that divided The University of Idaho and Washington State College. The annual football contest had become far more than just a game. It had become deeply embedded into the culture of these two communities where the winner could claim "bragging rights" over the other for the entire year. Neighbors with really no actual connection to either college would often align to one school or the other based on fan loyalty or family tradition. Idaho, the victor over Washington State more often than not (especially on their home field), knew its fans would be energized with a win over Washington State since it had suffered a losing season to date. While Washington State fans, riding on a winning streak, knew that rivalry games brought out the best in players, meaning all the speculation would mean nothing until the game was played. For decades, local fans grew up as a witness to how this annual game would divide friendships, divide communities, and turn even the most casual fan into a wild-eyed, raucous supporter.

Gambling was often commonplace, with entire teams making very public wagers, often boasting about odds given or terms offered. As far back as 1902, the University of Idaho team was so confident that it gave WSC 3-to-1 odds, resulting in an impressive fortune to bear of $3,000 (equivalent to $80,000 today). It wasn't easy for the Washington State players to raise the $1,000, but they did. In a surprising upset, WSC would win that game 17-0.

For days, fans on both sides had begun their celebrations. Bonfires were lit, hundreds of singing fans would form "serpentines" that would weave through town, often preventing anyone from getting past. Dozens of women in the Washington State Women's Athletic Association made plans to march the eight miles to the game wearing a special Washington State "fez" and blowing a "kazoo." Special rooter trains from all around the region would bring fans from both colleges to Moscow, Idaho, for the game.

All week long, Coach Dietz tried to keep a delicate balance between working his players into a new strategy for Idaho, all while giving them time to recuperate. Alfred Langdon had indeed separated his ribs. Asa Clark appeared to be at full strength, but was, in fact, masking shoulder pain. Fullback Carl Dietz had suffered most of the week from an ugly strain of the flu, while running back Benton Bangs seemed to enjoy the swagger that came with the black and blue marks healing around his eyes and cheekbones. Dietz knew he would be hard-pressed to keep any one player off the field for this cross-state rivalry game. After the Friday night rally, some thirty Idaho fans were caught trying to break into the Washington State locker room to steal the team's jerseys. Doc Bohler had anticipated the move, posting guards at the gym. After all, Idaho's jerseys had been stolen the year before.

Kick-Off

As the game was set to begin, the official count showed five-thousand fans had gathered for the largest crowd ever assembled for this border match-up. Temperatures were in the mid-70s. The crimson and gray sweaters of Washington State fans slightly overshadowed the black and yellow colors of The University of Idaho. After warm-ups, players made their way slowly to the sidelines. It was Clark who reacted angrily when Dietz told him to sit out for at least the first half. Bohler intervened, claiming the move was his idea. But Dietz knew it would be critical for keeping his captain healthy for the rest of the season.

Winning the coin toss, Washington State elected to receive the ball to start the game. As the teams prepared to kick off, Dietz looked across the field for any insight into new Idaho Head Coach Rademacher. Cut from the ballfields of Chicago, Rademacher had come to Idaho with several new players and an entirely new set of strategies. Dietz knew the team was set to have a breakout game. Like a master looking at a chessboard, Dietz scrutinized every player, every moment during warmups, seeking any advantage.

The sound of the Idaho fans reached a crescendo as the team delivered a high kick to begin the game. Washington State Quarterback Bull Durham would catch the short kick on his own 30-yard line and take off up the sidelines. But the Idaho defenders came with a fury, striking the quarterback so hard it looked as if he had slammed into a solid object. The ball popped loose, and Idaho would recover, causing its fans to cheer with a single, deafening voice. Durham got up slowly and headed to the sidelines. It would be a long day for the starting quarterback. Benton Bangs, on the other hand, sprinted back to the sidelines. You could tell there was a lot of pent-up energy in this speedy halfback. Dietz could see that energy, and he knew much of this day might just lie on his young running back's shoulders.

On the field, the Washington State defense responded with its tradition of confusing teams from the very start. Defenders were constantly on the move, leaving some blockers double-covered, and others wide-open. Idaho ran two plays without success. On third down, Idaho tried to sneak in an early reverse, but Washington State's Ron Fishback wasn't fooled, knocking down the Idaho back for a big loss. Despite picking up a fumble on the Washington State 30-yard line, Idaho found itself needing to punt without gaining any traction. Benton Bangs stood restlessly on the sidelines, shifting his weight left, then right, in eager anticipation.

This was the game he had truly prepared for his entire life.

Bangs

From his earliest days, Benton Bangs had loved to run. He remembered the exhilaration he felt running down the hill at his grandfather's apple farm in Chelan, Washington, darting back and forth through the apple trees, dodging tree branches that tried to reach out and grab him. On the football field, he now felt that same heady thrill as he crashed through linemen with a football in his hands.

Bangs looked into the stands for his father, a die-hard Washington State football fan who wouldn't have missed this game. When Bangs was a boy, every Wednesday evening when the weekly paper arrived, his father would regale his children with stories from the gridiron. The importance of the annual rivalry game between Idaho and his father's beloved team came alive as his father read aloud dispatches from each game.

As he raced out to the field alongside of his quarterback, Durham, Bangs made his nonverbal message—"give me the ball"—clear with the energy he brought to the field. Durham was only too happy to oblige since his team would take over the ball deep in their own territory. With a smile, Durham whispered a familiar cadence "Apple -3." Washington State's center, Langdon, snapped the ball perfectly into the hands of Bangs, who sprinted at full speed to his right. Quickly into Bangs' field of vision, the speedy freshman Ron Fishback, filling in for the injured Asa Clark, led the pack. The pulling lineman opened a hole that Bangs exploited to perfection, surprising the defenders by heading into open ground at full speed. In desperation, grabbing hands and bodies finally caught up with him, but not before he gained 35 yards.

First down, on Idaho's 35-yard line.

Washington State fullback, Carl Dietz, would get the ball next for a short gain, followed by a short pass to the end, Hanley. Bangs finished his blocking and jumped up quickly in front of Durham with the look athletes often deliver when they can see the outcome of a play before them before it even starts—a look that Durham believed. From the moment Bangs took the snap, time seemed to change. The sound of the crowd disappeared. Blockers moved in slow motion. The tree branches would not slow him this time. The back of the end zone was the only reason Bangs would stop. As he paused, the sound of the fans quickly caught up with him.

He had given his team a 7-0 lead.

On the sidelines, Coach Dietz greeted each of his players individually, shaking their hands. Despite the change of personnel, his team was still moving down the field with uncanny precision. But Dietz would not let his team rest just yet. He knew how quickly these rivalry games could rapidly change.

As Idaho went back on offense, it seemed unable to respond. The ever-changing front presented by Washington State left the Idaho players in a constant state of bewilderment, trying to figure out where to go and whom to block. From the stands, it must have appeared to fans that Idaho's players were somehow cast under a spell that left them stunned and unable to play. But in truth, Washington State had forced them into a game they had never experienced. Idaho would again be faced with the same frustration—three plays—three failed attempts to make any yardage, and Idaho would again have to punt.

Standing on the edge of the sidelines, Bangs had not spoken to anyone. Like a sprinter in the blocks, he shot out to take his place in the game. Durham saw the look in his halfback's eyes, and decided that if the series had worked once, it might work twice. This time, Bangs took off so quickly he nearly outran his blockers. It was as if he were in a completely different zone than anyone else on the field. Five times, Bangs went to the line with the ball. Each time, he erupted for runs of at least 5 yards and as many as 35. Once more over the right side, he again found himself in the end zone.

Washington State would have a 14-0 lead.

Pandemonium struck the Washington fan base, which surprisingly outnumbered the hometown crowd. Few had believed their boys could continue this winning streak, having suffered what seemed a lifetime of contests over the years where assured victory suddenly twisted into defeat. For fans on both sides, there was plenty on the line. The outcome of this game would be a constant source of taunting and one-upmanship for years to come.

As Idaho's defenders rose up to play offense, they again would find no answer—partially because they faced a Washington State defense where each man seemed as fresh as they did on first down. Idaho's offensive linemen were still gasping for breath after two relentless defensive stands without a break. On this series, Idaho was able to move the ball for a few plays, yet the end result was the same. Idaho would find itself punting again just as the first quarter came to an end.

Benton Bangs raced onto the field by himself, not realizing the quarter had ended. He had convinced Dietz to let him return the next punt, while trying to forget the fumble he had coughed up just a few weeks earlier. Silently, he stood during the entire break, waiting for his chance to run. When the teams returned to the field, Idaho got off a decent punt, but the ball seemed just to hang straight up in the air. A sprinting Bangs barely reached the ball before it hit the ground, catching it on his fingertips. Suddenly, there he was, running at full speed against a team just getting underway. Picking his way across the field, moving left, then quickly to the right, Bangs wound his way all the way down to the Idaho 15-yard line.

The first to greet him on the field was the quarterback, Durham, who smiled as he whispered the play: Bangs would get the ball straight up the middle. Washington State was ready to snap just as

Idaho was barely set. Bangs grabbed the Langdon snap perfectly on the dead run as blockers opened up enough space to shoot through. No branches would be there to catch him.

Just like that, WSC had taken a 21-0 lead.

As the crowd continued its uproar, two unexpected guests watched quietly in the stands: Jerry Nissen, the former WSC star and now the head coach at Montana, and "Wee" Doyle, the head football coach from Gonzaga, an enormous man whose name was a complete misnomer. Both coaches had also brought along a handful of players to get a glimpse of their upcoming foes.

Idaho was driving like a cart with a missing wheel. Nothing it did seemed to work. Idaho tried passing the ball, even tried to run a few trick plays, yet each one was rewarded with only a minimal gain. Meanwhile, the Washington State defense began substituting younger, less-experienced players.

Benton Bangs could not sit down. He remained poised on the edge of the sidelines, just waiting for his chance to get back into the game. He hardly noticed Carl Dietz, the fullback, who was panting like he had just come out of the game. Clearly, Carl was laboring from the past week's illness. The team was now working its way down the field with true efficiency. Not once had it changed its game plan, running the exact same plays as the series before. It was as if the team knew exactly what play to run without gathering back in a huddle, just popping right up and into the action as quickly as the plays had ended.

On the 3-yard line, Durham knew everyone would be focused on Bangs, who was having the game of his life. Smiling, Durham whispered the play to Langdon, his center. On the snap, Bangs shot ahead of the big fullback with a fake that pulled away most of the defenders. Instead, Carl Dietz, with the ball, would cross the finish line untouched; he would drop to the turf in sheer exhaustion as the half came to an end.

131

WSC led 28-0 at halftime, but Carl Dietz would not return.

Inside the locker room, players began to laugh and celebrate as if this game were over. Coach Dietz wondered whether this newfound swagger might grow dangerously close to overconfidence. But there was something else. His top players continued to show signs of serious wear and tear. Whatever speech he tried to make would be interrupted by a large roar of the crowd. Dietz told his players they would be rotating in plenty of the younger players in the second half, which did not sit well with his starters in this rivalry matchup. Coach Dietz also made plans to return to using a huddle in the second half to help chew up the clock.

As the players headed out, the coaches were met by excited fans, eager to let them know the announcement had been made: the team from the Oregon Agricultural College had just beaten the Michigan Aggies in convincing fashion, with the final score of 20-0. The news might not have sunk in immediately, but the victory would prove to have a profound impact on the Washington State team.

As promised, Asa Clark would take the field to start the second half, eliciting a round of applause from both sides of the field. The Idaho game was too important to miss. He gazed into the stands to see one Lillian McDonald, who had made it known she would walk the entire eight miles just to see him play.

Idaho answered strong to start the second half. A short kick by Washington State gave them the ball at mid-field. With that, Idaho went to work calling quick plays itself. A run-off right tackle worked for 5 yards, then a short run to the left netted 3 more. Morrison, the Idaho quarterback, with his own fake handoff, spun outside by himself for another 7 yards. Suddenly, Idaho had a first down on Washington's 35-yard line.

Whatever frivolity that had been carried onto the field from the half quickly vanished as Washington State finally settled in, holding

Idaho to just 4 more yards over the next three plays. Idaho's Dingle lined up for a field goal to put his team on the board. The kick was up, no—it was blocked! Washington State's defense would hold again.

Jubilant Washington State players all but danced off the field, met by an equally excited offensive unit. With the ball and a comfortable lead, Washington began to grind down the clock. A sweep around the right side for 10 yards was called back because of a holding penalty, and just like that, Washington State was facing third down and 20, from its own 25-yard line. Taking his time in the huddle, quarterback Bull Durham, with a smile, called a rare passing play. On the snap, Durham floated a pass out to the flat, not realizing that Idaho's Thompson had tracked the play, intercepting it on a dead run. Racing down the sideline, Bangs shot off from the backfield in a desperate attempt to catch him, only to trip him up on the 1-yard line. Just like that, Idaho was poised to score.

A more serious defensive unit raced back onto the field. Washington State had not given up a touchdown all season. Idaho lined up with a fierce determination. Of the attempt, the sports reporters would write, "Four times the mighty Idaho men tried their best to cross the final yard into the end zone. Four times, they were stopped cold by Washington State." Washington State's fans and players alike let go a collective sigh of relief.

The offense took to the field with an almost playful attitude. The hard-charging Basil Doane picked up where Carl Dietz had left off. But it was Benton Bangs who remained unstoppable. Running the ball again for five plays, covering 75 yards and another touchdown, Washington State had a commanding 35-0 lead. But celebrations on the play were short-lived as the rangy quarterback, Bull Durham, left the field holding his side. Somehow, during the extra point, he had gotten caught up in a pile of players and came up injured.

The defense stood its ground, forcing yet another Idaho punt. But with Washington State's Durham out, a surprised Clyde Boone was substituted into the game. Boone hadn't played quarterback since high school. But even with a slower pace and a lineup filled with players who hadn't seen much action this season, Washington State still moved the ball quickly and efficiently. At one point, the team even called out for a halfback pass. On the snap, Bangs shot off to the right with Idaho drawn in to the sweep. Dick Hanley slid outside into the spot normally taken by Durham. The pass, a wobbly one that seemed to take forever, landed softly into Hanley's hands, giving Washington State a 20-yard gain. On the next play, a fake to Bangs again left the fullback wide open for the touchdown. This time, the younger Doane marched the ball in. Bangs would try his hand at making a drop-kick that missed badly.

It didn't matter. Washington State would beat Idaho 41-0, in a score that was certain to remain lodged in the local folklore for decades to come. Benton Bangs had amassed an unprecedented 468 yards on the day and four touchdowns.

Several sports writers had spotted the visiting head coaches in the stands and asked what they thought of Bangs' performance; "In my estimation, Bangs ranks up there with the top three backs to ever play in the Northwest," said Gonzaga coach, Doyle. The sentiment was echoed by Montana coach, Jerry Nissen: "Bangs leads a team that is the strongest I have ever seen at Washington State College." While both men were quick to offer their praise, in truth, they were both privately plotting how to stop Bangs when their turn came around.

Back in the locker room, the mood was expectedly exuberant. These players had just won bragging rights for themselves and their fans for years to come in the area. Coaches knew this would be a moment that the players, and even themselves, would savor the rest of their days.

A New Voice

Roscoe Fawcett had long written about football for the Oregonian newspaper. His writing always seemed to find a unique perspective on the game. The Oregon Agricultural College victory over the Michigan Aggies in Lansing was a tremendous victory. Not just for the college's program, but for all football on the West Coast.

A long-standing sports tradition called "stacking" gave writers the opportunity to compare teams that had not played each other. OAC had beaten MAC 20-0, after MAC had beaten Michigan 24-0 a few weeks earlier. By adding them together, or "stacking," one could make the case that the Oregon Aggies were "better than Michigan." The OAC victory would have been sweeter had the team not fallen to Washington State the week before.

But that loss gave Roscoe an idea.

As he rolled his paper into the typewriter, he wrote out the words he had mulled the weekend long. Roscoe typed a bold pronouncement, "Washington State College has the best football team in all America, barring none." Pausing, Roscoe had to smile. He could already hear the howling from Seattle fans over his headline. Yet Roscoe was a well-respected columnist who knew well how to craft a story.

On a roll now, Roscoe supported his claim: "I have reached this conclusion after reading through the scores from games played thus far both East and West." Falling back on his old tried-and-true stacking, Roscoe continued "Washington State College beat the Oregon Aggies 29-0; The Oregon Aggies beat the Michigan Aggies 20-0; the Michigan Aggies beat Michigan U 24-0; ergo Washington State College is 73-points better than Michigan."

By the time Roscoe was done, he had stacked in teams from all over the East Coast, proclaiming WSC to be better than most of the Eastern powerhouses such as Syracuse, Harvard, Cornell, and Yale. For years, these Eastern teams had dominated the national sports discussion. When his paper came out on Monday, in towns like Portland and Seattle, there was sure to be plenty of talk.

Washington State College had officially arrived onto a national stage.

Pullman

Sunday afternoon was the only time visitors were allowed at sororities at Washington State College. At the Pi Beta Phi house, two young women were especially eager this day since each was expecting a visit from a player on the suddenly popular football team. Both Lillian McDonald and Helen Quarrels were busy putting on their makeup, having spent the entire morning making sure their best dresses were at the ready.

The head mistress' voice rang up the staircase. "Lillian, you have a gentleman caller." Lillian dropped everything and gazed into the mirror, hoping she looked just how she wanted. Glancing at the clock, she realized her visitor was nearly thirty minutes early. Although worried that her hair wasn't as perfect as it could be, she would not keep Asa Clark waiting.

Calming herself, she walked from the room with her most practiced poise and down the stairs, showing as much grace as possible. This was, of course, a gentleman calling. From the top of the stairs, she could see the man's shoes all shiny and well cared for, while his dark gray suit was impeccably tailored. Pulling away her gaze, so as not to appear too eager, Lillian glided down the stairs, pausing only at the end to make a slow, welcoming turn.

She was face to face with an all too familiar gentlemen; it was "Slats" Olson.

Visiting Day

If Asa Clark was nervous, it didn't show. The last twenty-four hours had been exciting enough with the win over cross-border rival Idaho. After all, how difficult could it be to visit a young woman for the first time? He wouldn't be alone in his visit to the Pi Beta Phi house. Benton Bangs, dressed nicely on his day off, joined him on his walk. Neither one should have been surprised to see the other. After all, they had both been to the same dance.

Panic

Lillian was frozen. Her face portrayed a look of sheer panic. "Slats," as his fellow baseball players in town called him, was not someone she was expecting. Her true suitor would be at the door any moment. Slats had been a casual acquaintance of Lillian's who seemed to keep coming back despite her dismissive attitude toward him.

The house mother, keen to the goings on within her house, knew what to do. Intervening, she politely asked the young gentlemen to leave, given that Lillian had a caller scheduled to arrive. As she guided him toward the door, she glanced back to see a still frozen Lillian, and she gave her a quiet nod of the head, as if to say, "I have this under control." In response, Lillian turned on her heels and raced back up the staircase.

The house mother stepped away, believing the young man would show himself out. But Slats Olson, who had quite the feelings for young Lillian, was filled with both surprise and curiosity. Pausing, he realized the house mother had moved away. So he only pretended to leave, ducking into the parlor instead.

Looking about, he saw there were very few places one could hide.

A knock on the door had Slats looking back and forth in a panic. He could hear the voice of the head mistress welcoming a visitor at the door. Quickly, he tried to wrap himself behind the curtain, but he quickly learned there wasn't as much space as he had thought. Just as the gentlemen moved into the room, Slats did the only thing possible; he ducked down behind the couch.

Arrival

After a firm knock on the door, Asa Clark was surprised to see the sorority door open quickly, as if someone had been waiting on the other side for his arrival. It was the head mistress there to meet Bangs and him. With a proper greeting of the two gentlemen callers, the house mother was at the ready. Mr. Clark would be escorted into the parlor, while Mr. Bangs would be taken into the nearby sitting room.

With that, Bangs and the house mother disappeared, leaving Clark to wander into the room by himself. Out of the corner of his eye, he caught a glimpse of a figure gliding down the staircase. Lillian, now well-rehearsed in her entrance, paused just above the bottom stair and turned slowly to meet the gaze of her suitor.

With a surprise, she let out a gasp.

Clark smiled to himself at the reaction, but in reality, Lillian had seen the familiar blondish-red hair of Slats Olson popping back down behind the couch. Clark walked to the edge of the staircase and extended his hand to guide her to the couch.

Lillian must have looked at him blankly, not knowing what to do.

Clark had plenty to talk about. The rivalry game had become the talk of campus. But for Lillian, a full conversation must have been nearly impossible. It would have been difficult at best to talk while trying not to glance back behind the couch, knowing their every word was heard by the hidden suitor. The last thing she needed was to explain what "Slats" was doing hiding behind the couch.

As the conversation wrapped up, the two made plans to see each other the following week. If Asa Clark thought the conversation stilted, he never made mention of it, being simply pleased to receive the promise of another meeting yet to come. As Clark stood to leave, the somewhat quiet and demur Lillian displayed a completely different side. When Clark turned to shake her hand, Lillian all but jumped forward to give him a lingering kiss on the cheek.

The move surprised them both.

Clark smiled, and then he made his way out the door. Picking up his pace, he began to whistle, but then he paused a moment to listen more carefully. Shaking his head, he laughed at his imagination. He could swear he heard a woman's voice yelling angrily inside the sorority house.

CHAPTER 5

MONTANA

MONTANA

Pullman, Washington
November 6, 1915

Any football coach will tell you that one of the most difficult tasks he faces is convincing a young man to play above himself, convincing him to push past the pain of injury or fatigue because victory does not give you permission to relax. Players, by their very nature, often default back to what is least expected of them. It is human nature. Yet there is no time to rest on your laurels before any game is finished. Dietz knew he needed to get these players past their own successes and motivate them to be more than they had before. For sunrise Monday morning, he had called a special practice session—a reminder there was still plenty of work to do.

Preparations

Montana Coach Jerry Nissen had his own ideas on how to beat Washington State. Two of his biggest players had been part of the alumni game. Their success gave the coach pause to believe sheer brute force could push the smaller and speedier team out of the way. Tiny Keeran and Fane Vance had played football for the 1913 WSU team and had followed Coach Nissen to Montana. It didn't hurt that each of them now tipped the scaled at over 235-pounds each. Nissen himself had been the Captain of the Washington State team back in 1908.

What few knew was that Nissen brought most of his players to the Idaho game and hid them among the crowd so they could see this new team operate for themselves. Nissen's plan was simple. Line up his players in a tight formation so that when the lighter Washington State players tried to bunch them up, he would have the size just to push them out of the way. On defense, the coach had just the opposite idea. Line his biggest men to the outside and then push everything to the inside. It would give his defense a distinct advantage in the inside running game, while making the running backs go farther to the outside.

With this new approach, they believed they had found Washington State's Achilles' heel.

Rose Bowl Selection

The deadline was rapidly approaching.

A.J. Bertonneau had convinced the Rose Bowl committee it would need to extend invitations to teams weeks in advance in order to have negotiations completed by Thanksgiving. His committee of business leaders, sportsmen, and one former coach had been brought together to select just who would be the best two teams in the nation to compete in their new football championship.

Picking a clear leader from the East proved to be a difficult task. No one team had that signature win needed to capture the hearts and imagination of sports fans. From the East, Cornell and Pittsburgh were both intriguing choices. Each was so far undefeated. Pittsburgh was led by Pop Warner, the former Carlisle coach, offering a match-up of a coach versus student. The problem was that Pittsburgh only had one key win over Pennsylvania. Cornell had the same issue with one signature win over Harvard. Yale had long been the team to beat in the East, with a win over Princeton.

Time was proving to be of the essence. The committee would reconvene the next week in hopes of determining which team to invite. A lot was riding on this decision. Making the right match-up would be critical in their plans to attract upwards of 40,000 fans to their annual event.

Infirmary

A flu bug had descended on Washington State College. A rash of faculty members and senior students reported coming down with heavy cold symptoms to the college nurse. All of them had registered on the college's official "sick list." The outbreak concerned the local nurses who served as administrators for the school. The current remedy for most cases was a bottle of "Old Crow" whiskey, said to help ease symptoms and suffering so people could sleep. Given that Pullman was a "dry" town, nurses worried about getting enough supplies to help out during this crisis.

In fact, the head nurse, Ida Mae Keane, spoke to President Bryan about how proud she was to see those afflicted continuing their daily lives. "You wouldn't know it from seeing them, but we really do have a lot of people out there suffering." In considering her request for more "medicine," the president likely only smiled, while asking her to "do her best."

Game Day

Weather in Pullman can be a tricky thing in the fall. Sometimes, the winter sets in quickly with no sign of letting go. Other years, like this one in 1915, the warm air covers you like a soft blanket. It was to be such a warm, sunny day for today's match-up with Montana. The weather matched Coach Dietz's outlook. He loved the fact that his team looked healthy, rested, and ready. His team's entire week had been spent running, lots and lots of running. Not just wind sprints, but using every moment to rehearse plays, running them at full speed. What he didn't do was scrimmage the team. What he lost in their physical strength from such an exercise, he gained back in healing up a number of potentially serious injuries.

What Dietz didn't have an answer for was the sheer size of

Montana's two big linemen. While the program listed them as 235 pounds, they were each easily forty pounds larger than that, and strong to boot. Dietz realized the only way to win was to neutralize their threat. Well, at least half of it anyway. The plan was for Asa Clark to line up one-on-one with the biggest man on the field, Tiny Keeran, and on every down, drive straight into the big man. Dietz knew the only chance was to wear the big man down. The only relief Clark would get would be from the occasional substitution from Fishback.

Whatever whimsical thoughts about Lillian McDonald that Clark may have brought into the day likely disappeared when he stepped onto the field. He was about to face the biggest challenge of his football career.

Anticipation

In the stands, Lillian McDonald settled in next to her friend, Helen Quarrels. The two no longer sat with their fellow Pi Beta Phi sisters. They had been elevated to seats up close, reserved by players in the game. Lillian had been seeing much more of her handsome captain, while Helen had put her hooks into one Benton Bangs.

Bangs had become the talk of campus. The town leaders had nominated him for All-American honors after his performance the week before against Idaho.

Kick-Off

At the very last minute, the Washington State players pulled off their jerseys and slipped on an entirely new set of game wear—fancy slick fabric, made of the same cotton and silk blend used by the pros. Their sleeves sported a combination of colors in alternating rings. On their backs—something no Washington State team had ever done before—each jersey had been numbered. It had been all Doc Bohler's doing. An anonymous donor had come to him, insisting that he order only the best, adding, "If these men play like champions, then by golly they need to look like champions." The uniforms had arrived just the day before. While the donor has never been identified, plenty of speculation suggests President Enoch Bryan may have had a hand in rewarding these football warriors.

A coach must not only prepare his players, but prepare himself. While fans on the field witness a collision of two forces, nuances of the game are seen only by the two coaches on the sidelines. Watching whom the opposing coach talks with, or how quickly he substitutes a player can be as telling as any formation on the field. Dietz knew that the crafty coach on the opposing sideline would try to beat his men with sheer force. After all, that's what he would do himself. So Dietz's new strategy for this game was to match up his players with as much force as he could muster. A dangerous strategy because in essence he was betting his players could wear down the other team—faster than they could wear his men down. At left tackle, Asa Clark was now lined up against the largest man on the Montana team. Right next to him, Ron Fishback—the biggest man on the State team—was lined up at left guard. The crafty quarterback, Bull Durham, stood on the sidelines. Instead, two fullbacks were in the backfield: Carl Dietz and the hard hitting "Base" Doane. Benton Bangs was not in the backfield, but he had lined up on the right side at flanker. At the last minute, the taller Clarence Zimmerman came in to stand next to Clark at an end position, but he moved in next to the tackle, forming a three-man wall of Washington State's biggest and strongest men.

At the snap, the ball seemed to go straight up into the air. Both fullbacks shot off to the right, ignoring the ball. Montana's men had practiced taking a half-step backwards to avoid the body roll block, only to find themselves against an opponent that was coming right at them with straightforward blocking. Asa Clark shot off the line, driving his head right into the chest of Tiny Keeran. It was a block that would have driven any man to the ground, but not Keeran. The larger man grabbed onto Clark's shoulders and tossed him aside like a rag doll. Right next to him, Alfred Langdon shot out at Vance. On the line, the Montana defenders tried desperately to push ahead as the ball seemed to float into the air with an assured fumble. But on a dead run, the speedy Benton Bangs grabbed the ball and sprinted as fast as he could to the left side. The play would gain 9 yards. As quick as the play ended, the team had jumped back into position for another go. Each of these players had been practicing the first five plays in a row all week and knew what to expect without even pausing to speak.

Montana seemed ready. This time, the ball was snapped directly to Carl Dietz, who drove into the line on the left side. Montana's Keeran shook off the block and brought a hammering arm down across the body of the fullback that forced him to fumble. Fortunately, Washington State's own lineman, Ray Loomis, was able to recover. The team jumped up to get back into the play, but a whistle from the referee stopped play. Basil Doane was lying on the ground in pain, holding his right knee. He had twisted it badly trying to stop "Buster" Vance, who had blown through his blocker. On the sideline, Dietz knew this was going to be a tough matchup. The blocking duties would now land on the shoulders of his freshman Ralph Boone.

On the next play, Bangs grabbed the ball again out of mid-air and raced over the left side for a solid gain only to have a big hit by Keeran knock the ball loose. Fortunately, Bangs's forward momentum kept him up with the ball and he recovered. Running the exact same play would have the exact same result. Once again, the ball came loose, only this time Keeran grabbed Bangs's jersey and Montana would get the ball on the Washington State half of the field.

But Montana would get another surprise. There would be no mass substitution on defense. Coach Dietz looked like he was going to play his boys both directions. Asa Clark lined up directly in front of Tiny Keeran on defense. Clark knew his one and only job was to make the day miserable for Keeran, and he was just getting started.

Montana had thought it had practiced for the speedy Washington State defense. What it didn't understand was the unpredictable nature of its design. Players lined up ready to charge forward, only to disappear when the ball was snapped. In other cases, defenders acted like they were the ones doing the tackling, with rolling blocks knocking the offense off its feet and creating a pile-up that made it nearly impossible to move. The movement kept Montana off balance. On the first play, an offensive lineman moved too early for a 5-yard penalty. Running up the middle was no good. Montana tried going left, then right, but the speedy defenders just closed the ground too quickly and in large numbers.

Three plays and Montana would be punting. Yet on every play, no matter where it was going, Clark shot off his stance on the snap and drove himself into Keeran. Keeran had been knocked back on his heels. It was only for an instant, but it was enough to tell Clark that this immovable mountain of a man had his own weakness—that of stamina.

Montana's punt was a beauty, pinning Washington State back on its own 7-yard line. But WSC's offense could still not get going. Three running plays later—it was time for State to give back the ball. A low kick gave Montana the ball in solid field position at mid-field. After three running attempts, Montana found itself on a fourth down on Washington State's 20-yard line. Coach Nissen opted to go for a field goal, but the drop kick would land funny and the kick would miss wide. Washington State would take over on offense, having just dodged a bullet.

On the sideline, Coach Dietz was busy tending to his own worries. His substitutions would be few these first series. His big three horses—Zimmerman, Clark, and Fishback—had yet to leave the field. Langdon had come out for a few plays, yet insisted on going back into the game.

Montana would hold firm on the next series, despite Washington

State pressuring the defense by running play after play in rapid succession without much time for a break. Carl Dietz moved back to take the snap to punt, but he looked over to the left and realized Montana had only two men on the left side. As the play began, Clark continued his wrestling match with Keeran, while Zimmerman and Fishback held firm. The center, Alfred Langdon, also drove into Keeran, and then dropped to throw a body roll into the pursuing Vance.

That was when Carl decided to do something entirely of his own making. Oh, sure, Coach Dietz and he had talked about taking opportunities like this when they became available, but no player wants to risk messing things up. Glancing left, Carl Dietz acted quickly, grabbed the snap out of the air, and took off running through the hole left between his team's giants. In an instant, the fullback broke free and was racing down the side of the field, entirely unchecked. For Carl Dietz, everything seemed to freeze in time. The sound of the crowd disappeared. The only thing he could hear was the pulsing of his own breath. The moment came rushing back into focus when a speedy safety from Montana had just enough momentum from the side to push Carl out of bounds.

As Carl popped back up to run to the line of scrimmage, the cheer of the crowd quickly returned. His gamble had paid off. Glancing over to his coach, he didn't know how to read him. It was the perplexing look of a man who was joyful, yet stoic at the same time. As the quarter came to an end, a smiling Carl Dietz raced to receive the welcoming handshakes and moments of joy from his teammates. The play had given them an infusion of excitement.

Quarterback Bull Durham came onto the field to begin the second quarter. It was time to get back to their usual offense. Coach Dietz decided he'd had enough of trying to slug it out; now he wanted to test how his team would fair against a weary opponent. "Apple-3!" Durham called out as the players came up to the line of scrimmage. What was once a single play was now a play with five options. Bangs shot to the right side for a gain of 5 yards. Boone, now in for Dietz, gave the team a pair of lighter running backs. He headed over to the left side for 4 yards. Back and forth the team began to weave its offense. Soon it found itself down to the Montana goal line, where the boys from Montana called timeout.

As the Washington State players stood in a huddle, Clark signaled he had the big Montana lineman on the ropes. Believing he could push the giant back 1 yard, Durham made the call. The run could be right behind Clark.

On the snap, Clark shot straight out at Keeran, driving his head into the bigger man's chest. The stronger Keeran tried to use his arm strength to push Clark away—but this time, the Washington State captain just kept driving him backwards. The best Keeran could do was reach around Clark as Washington's running back, Benton Bangs, lowered his head and followed Clark into the end zone.

Washington State would have a 6-0 lead.

Durham, who hadn't played much, kept it a secret that he was still in a lot of pain. His drop kick missed to the right, but the fans didn't seem to mind. Their team was up by a touchdown to the mighty men from Montana.

Back on the sidelines, Coach Nissen saw how Washington State wanted to play match-up football and was more than happy to oblige. Nissen pulled his line in close together, with the plan to let his strong back Vance push forward, looking for a gap. What made Vance such a great runner was his ability to sprint outside when the middle was clogged up. The new offensive scheme began to work. Montana slowly moved the ball down the field. Nothing fancy, but the slow and steady march was proving to be effective. Right, then left, then up the middle, the team marched the ball to midfield until it looked like they would be stopped. On fourth down, Coach Nissen made a bold call—a fake run up the middle that was actually a bootleg pass. The ball was tossed to the speedy outside receiver, Doug Robertson, a track runner and Montana's fastest athlete. Robertson broke outside for nearly a 20-yard gain to the Washington State 25-yard line.

There are defining moments in every game, and for Washington State, this would be theirs. So far this season, the defense had kept the ball out of the end zone. And so it was that the Washington State men would dig in their heels. Three failed running attempts by Montana and a wild pass when the quarterback was scrambling for his life gave Washington State back the ball inside its own 20-yard line.

This time, Washington State went back to its dual fullback set, hoping to gain some traction. But Montana seemed to have figured out all of Washington State's plays. Three plays, and on fourth down, it was time to punt. No one noticed that Benton Bangs had stayed in the game, standing in the backfield as an apparent blocker in the punt formation. But on the snap, Bangs shot to the left and grabbed the ball out of mid-air. Driving through the exact same spot that Carl had earlier discovered, Bangs raced down the field for 55 yards before being stopped. A gutsy call had just taken away any momentum Montana had temporarily won.

Three more attempts would come up empty. Durham was back on the field for the drop kick—but again, it would miss. Washington still held a lead, 6-0.

On the sidelines, Dietz was watching carefully to see how the Montana team was holding up. He would need to give his big horses rest soon. Substituting for Zimmerman and Fishback, he decided to leave Clark and Langdon in the game. So far, it appeared each man had battled his opponent to a draw.

Montana took over with a vengeance. Its straight ahead style was gaining traction, especially with Dietz resting two of his best defenders. With a workman-like quality, Montana showed why they were among the best in the game. They marched right back down the field to the Washington 20-yard line. But Dietz's boys once again held tight. Montana's own drop kick would come up short.

Coach Dietz decided to leave his big horses on the sideline to rest until after halftime, which was rapidly approaching with just three minutes to play. He put his ailing quarterback into the game with hopes of keeping the plays simple in order to get the team into halftime to regroup.

It should have been simple enough.

Washington State tried three running plays to wind down the clock; then with forty-five seconds left, the team would need to punt. But football is a deceitful mistress. Just when you think you have her figured out, she decides to intervene at the hands of her partner "fate." A smaller WSC substitute player, Silas Stites, was knocked flat by a charging Claude McQuarrie, who easily blocked Carl's punt. The ball, after scrambling in the air, would roll behind clear to the 1-yard line. Montana's Clark would win the footrace to the ball and carry it into the end zone just as the half came to an end.

It would be the first time in five games the defense had given up a touchdown.

More importantly, it gave Montana a 7-6 lead at the half. Both fans and players were stunned by the sudden reversal.

Inside the locker room, the players didn't know how Coach Dietz would react. Would he be angry? No, that wasn't his nature. Would he feel victimized by luck? Instead, Coach Dietz did what the best of leaders do in times of great adversity. He walked casually in and smiled, not at all betraying the panic that had welled-up inside him. Dietz may have had good reason to be confident. As the half ended, he saw a weakness appearing in the Montana machine.

When the half had finished, Tiny Keeran and Buster Vance both sat down on the field to rest, while the rest of the Montana team was busy celebrating its sudden reversal of fortune.

Dietz chose to stick with his game plan.

Second Half

There are moments on the field of battle when a general knows his forces have the upper hand. A defending general will often press forward with hopes that some miracle will develop, but miracles rarely, if ever, do. And so it was with this game entering the second half. Montana's players walked back slowly to the field, despite having the lead. Washington State hit the field holding the upper hand when it came to conditioning. Even Asa Clark appeared to be energized. Going back to its original offense, Washington State took the ball in the second half, engaging in sweep after sweep, using body roll blocks to take out its opponents and move the ball at will. While on defense, it continued to move around and attack any weak spot it encountered.

On its second possession of the half, Benton Bangs sprinted around the right side to find that none of the Montana men could catch up. Weaving his way through a pack of six defenders with ease would give Washington State its first touchdown. Durham's pains subsided enough for an extra point to make the game 13-7.

It seemed as if a completely different Montana team now took the field. Nothing it did seemed to work. Passes were rushed and incomplete because of the speedy onslaught of Washington State. Runs were stopped cold. Washington State, taking full advantage of the lighter, more agile style, suddenly just kept rolling up the yards, marching down the field with ease, not just one more time but twice. The fullback, Dietz, and the backup, Boone, would both find their way into the end zone.

Final score—Washington State College 27, Montana 7.

The fans stayed for every minute. The first half had given many of them a scare that their boys had finally met their match. But the second half proved that the dream was still alive. A euphoria fills fans when a shared victory comes, especially when it's from a team that has not enjoyed such a sweet taste of success as at that very moment. Sports writers were quick to note that Washington State's very next game would bring the boys from Whitman to town. Writers began to hint that a lax schedule by the University of Washington, which refused to play many of the teams in the Northwest, would mean that a Washington State win would guarantee the team a conference victory.

This Cinderella story was still alive.

Washington

University of Washington coach Gil Dobie always seemed to find a way to be angry.

On the train ride back to Seattle, he should have been jubilant now that his team had just beaten California in Berkeley by an unbelievable margin of 72-0. He had yet to be defeated on the field. But his fans kept finding a way to despise him. For reasons he never understood, he was constantly barraged by peanut shells as the game wore on. What angered many fans the most was how Washington seemed to be avoiding teams of any prowess. California had never really had much of a team. It had only recently started a football program, stepping aside from its traditional rugby play. Yet despite this new program, California had agreed to come to Seattle as well, meaning it would play the University of Washington boys twice in one season. Washington's schedule had also included lightweight opponents such as club teams like the Ballard Meteors and Washington Park A.C.

The number of fans attending the games had dwindled to under two thousand.

Sports writers began to raise questions about this upstart Washington State team. Coach Dietz had been quoted saying, "I know how to beat Dobie." Several reporters had been pressing for a game to be added between the two sides. Colorado wasn't helping matters at all by offering to forego coming to Seattle for its Thanksgiving Day game. Winter storms had already settled into the mountains there, making travel difficult this time of year.

Dinner

Lillian McDonald couldn't understand what was going on with her beau Asa Clark. She had arranged for him and several teammates to join the sorority for a special dinner this Saturday evening after the game. It wasn't too hard to convince Mr. Bangs to attend. Surely, this would be a happy occasion.

But Asa Clark seemed sullen, and deep in thought. He had barely touched his soup. All he would do was stare into his plate as if somehow it was far more entertaining than the company around him. Lillian tried her best to engage him in conversation. But after one pointed question his way, Clark reacted by not saying a word. Slowly, he looked up and gazed into Lillian's eyes. His silence caused her briefly to panic. Had she said something to offend him? As if in slow motion, he broke his gaze and returned to staring back into his bowl. Lillian placed her hand on Clark's shoulder. But the physical contact was enough to cause Asa Clark slowly to lean left and fall out of his chair, unconscious, onto the floor.

Recovery

Coach Dietz knew his team was hurting. Durham was not yet back to full strength. Doane's knee was pretty swollen up. Hanley was still suffering from a late shoulder separation. Dietz decided to write a note to the team that he wanted to be passed around and initialed by everyone before it was returned to his office.

"Congratulations to the best team in the Northwest," wrote Dietz.

"Our contest this weekend will be for the championship. I will need you rested and ready. We will not hold practice again until Thursday. Instead, I wish for you to spend time recovering, eating well, perhaps some light running and to catch up on your school work. I will see you again on Thursday afternoon as we prepare for this final home match of the season."

He signed it, "The Coach of the greatest team in the land, William Lone Star Dietz."

Dietz smiled as he placed the note in an envelope to give to Doc Bohler.

He turned his attention to something more relaxing. He had been asked to give a lecture to the Architectural Club this Thursday on "The Influence of Art and Music on Architecture."

Exhaustion

Doc Bohler had sprinted across the campus and into the Pi Beta Phi house, having been summoned by an out-of-breath young football player. Inside, he found Asa Clark lying on the couch in the parlor where his team had placed him. His collar had been loosened to help him breathe. Bohler dropped to Clark's side and grabbed his hand to feel his pulse. Concern on Bohler's face briefly eased; the pulse was strong and steady. As he turned to open his bag for his stethoscope, Bohler froze, caught off guard by a strange breathing sound. Leaning in closer, he strained to understand what he was hearing.

It was snoring.

Doc Bohler's shoulders visibly sagged, the tension of the moment fleeting. Smiling to himself, he put his equipment away. A teammate nearby asked, "What is it, Doc? Will he be O.K.?"

"Nothing that a good night's sleep won't cure," answered the doctor as he got up to leave. Asa Clark would not wake up for the next twenty-four hours. The exhaustion of the game had taken its toll. Clark's body had finally given in to the events of the day.

Selection

The Tournament of Roses football selection committee appeared to be narrowing its focus to a handful of teams from the East. With an air of uncertainty about the record on the season thus far, and with the rest of the season yet to be played, the tournament selection committee was forced to base its choice on reputation. Consideration was given to several schools, including Syracuse, Michigan, and Carlisle, each of which presented its own set of challenges.

In the end, it came down to a single football game. Brown University had just knocked off Yale in one of the biggest football upsets of the season. The team was an intriguing, and defendable, choice, with key wins earlier in the season over Vermont and Williams. But the team wasn't without problems, having lost to Syracuse 6-0 and to Amherst 7-0. Yet Brown offered something else—Fritz Pollard, an enormous player said to have the strength of ten men, among the very first African-Americans to play college football.

That was all the committee needed. The vote was cast to invite Brown University to represent the East. The team would be traveling all the way from its home state of Rhode Island, with hopes of bringing along plenty of fans and excitement to fill the stands for an entire week of activities.

Brown University president William Faunce wasted little time in accepting, but he would need to wait for more than a week to make the invitation public. The committee still needed to find a West Coast champion.

CHAPTER 6
WHITMAN

WHITMAN

Pullman, Washington
November 13, 1915

The November weather on the Palouse began to reveal its colder side, as temperatures quickly fell below freezing. *The Farmer's Almanac* had seemed fairly convinced this snow-filled season would begin with "light sprinkles" before Thanksgiving.

Football had reached a fervor pitch in the region. A group of business leaders decorated roads coming into Pullman from Spokane, Walla Walla, and Lewiston, Idaho, with Crimson and Gray roadside markers. Along the way, drivers would read the simple phrase: "The crimson and gray trail leads to Pullman." There was something about the team that seemed to cross all party lines, all ages even crossing traditional rivalries.

The unity the college so needed in the region continued to grow. WSC President Enoch Bryan's vision had come to completion and none-too-soon, as Bryan had agreed to step down at the end of this year. Already, his replacement had been selected; Ernest Holland was a Harvard trained administrator who spoke the language and held the respect of his Ivy League peers. Despite his years of toil to build and defend Washington State College, Bryan's most public legacy was rapidly becoming football.

In the newspapers of the day, articles began to surface praising the Washington State team. *The Spokane Daily Chronicle* began to cover the team, even writing how Coach Dietz casually walked the sideline with a unique style of running the team. Yet it was a measured sense of respect, referring to Dietz as a "red-skinned aborigine." Dietz would not react to such characterizations. He had dealt with them his entire life.

Warmups

Coach Dietz again decided to keep practice light. So long as the weather remained cold, there would be no scrimmaging. Dietz specifically left out any reference to winning the league championship to his players. Yet it was a factor paramount in the minds of sports writers around the Northwest. One bright spot—the team's captain, Asa Clark, was back on the practice field, despite having collapsed over dinner the previous weekend.

In keeping with Dietz treating his team like champions, players were met by a surprise addition. Doc Bohler opened up a special box containing dozens of new leather gloves, each thinly made, with soft leather and coated with a light oil to help keep them waterproof. The fingers and the palms were rough, while the outer edges were smooth. The gloves would help in the week ahead, especially with freezing temperatures expected for Saturday's game. Leather gloves were a true treat, usually reserved for the most elite in society. Yet here was a custom set of gloves made especially for keeping hands warm, yet thin enough for players to "feel" the ball with leather to hold in the heat. Not only were the gloves rare, but neither the players nor the coaches had ever heard of them before.

Fans

In the midst of all the chaos of last Saturday's game, Asa Clark took note of something he hadn't seen before—extremely rude fans from Washington State. Oh sure, there was plenty of renewed enthusiasm with the team performing well on the field. But some of the fans' actions bordered on being abusive.

Just after the Idaho game, numerous reports were made of fist fights breaking out between rival fans. Players were just hearing about some of the shenanigans. A telegram had been sent by a group of fans after the OAC game to former WSC football coach, John Bender, now coaching at Missouri. The telegram had basically shamed the former coach by saying how Dietz had found a way to win with the exact same team that Bender had coached the year before.

Further reports said that during the Montana game, several WSC fans had gathered on the sidelines behind the visiting team calling out, "Go Montana! Go Montana!" using a falsetto that made them sound like young girls. In response, the Washington State side answered back with a derogatory "Give 'em hell, Washington! Give 'em hell." Clark decided he needed to make his feelings known publically, so he wrote a letter to the editor, asking for fans to behave. "Every man on the team would appreciate very much if the rooters would treat the visitors in the very best manner possible." Clark did not believe Oregon or Montana teams were treated well, going so far as to call out his own fans for being unsportsmanlike. His fear was that word would spread, making it tough for road games in the future. "These schools may treat us in the same way when we play return games," Clark wrote.

From the WSC student newspaper, *The Evergreen*

> Sophomore Arthur Daniels of LaCrosse is healing well after suffering from a broken jaw during the Freshman/ Sophomore tie-up contest. Daniels is not expected to return to school until next year. Both classes have agreed to share the costs of Daniel's medical bill. The freshman class has voted to give $30, while the sophomore class has kicked in the final $20. Leaders from both classes felt it was wrong for the teen to both suffer from the misfortune of the event and suffer from the medical bills as well.

Kick-Off

The mild temperatures the week before now gave way to a bitter cold spell—such was the weather found on the Palouse. Damp rains during the week had turned the field into a sheet of ice, while the players arrived to an early morning four-inch blanket of snow. After winning the toss, WSC elected to receive.

Given the extremely slick conditions, Bangs could do little but catch the ball on the team's 40-yard line, where Washington State would begin its march. Sliding into the three back set that the team used so well against Montana, the team lined up with freshman Basil Doane alongside the speedy Benton Bangs and behind fullback Carl Dietz, who had become one of the most durable players on the field. But the game was far from pretty. On one of the first plays, Benton Bangs swung around the right side, only to fumble the ball and recover the ball himself—three times. It would be the last time he wore the special leather and canvas gloves they had been given.

Fans jumped and sang to keep warm. Their spirits were high as their boys marched the ball down the field in a drive that ended with Carl Dietz crossing the goal line for the touchdown. With ease, Washington State was ahead of the Whitman Missionaries 7-0.

Hanging on to the ball became a true problem for both sides. Whitman's first attempt at running the ball also ended up in a fumble. Washington State would not be on offense very long, returning the favor by coughing up the ball inside Whitman's 10-yard line. Both sides seemed to be struggling just to stay on their feet.

In the second quarter, the game bordered on becoming ridiculous, with snow becoming so hard-packed that players danced as if on an ice-skating rink. The only highlight was on an end around run when Benton Bangs picked up two Whitman defenders, who held on desperately to make the play, only to have Bangs tow them down the field. The play elicited a number of laughs and catcalls from his fellow teammates. Even the serious Coach Dietz had to allow himself a smile on that one. A few plays later, the mood on the sidelines turned to giddiness as Carl Dietz finished a short five-play drive, diving in untouched for the second score, sliding all the way out of the end zone.

Washington State would end the first half with a 14-0 lead.

Heading into the locker room, Coach Dietz noticed that his counterpart had already begun to substitute younger players. For Whitman, the game, for all intent, was over.

As Coach Dietz walked into the room, he found a completely different attitude from what he had seen before; where early games had these men steadfastly serious about the rest of the game to come, this time there was a true sense of frivolity. Dietz announced that a number of the younger players would be taking over in the second half. He wanted his players healthy for their last contest of the year—Dietz had devised a plan to play the University of Washington on Thanksgiving Day.

Second Half

The comedy continued well into the second half. By the time this game was over, a record of seventeen fumbles would officially be recorded. But in truth, many, many more had not gone into the official count. Whitman gave Washington State one scare in the fourth quarter when it marched down the field to the 20-yard line, only to fumble the ball away.

Basil Doane, now called "Digger" by his teammates, took over most of the running duties in the second half and appeared to have broken wide open on a sweep around the right, only to get up a full head of steam and then promptly fall flat on his face. Ray Loomis, who saw considerable playing time in the place of Clarence Zimmerman, had two interceptions on the day, but was kept on the sidelines following a nasty blow to the head.

With time running out, Washington State had the ball on the Whitman 38-yard line. Durham, who hadn't played, came up to the coach, wanting to know whether the team could try a long field goal. Dietz could only look at his young quarterback. Certainly Durham had the leg for it. It just wasn't something the team had tried before. With the game in hand, and some doubt whether a drop kick might work given the icy conditions, Coach Dietz gave the go ahead. After all, it would be the last play of the game.

Racing onto the field, Durham called his team together for his longest attempt ever. At the snap, Whitman's defenders just stood up, almost daring Durham to pull it off. The quarterback paused to make sure he had the ball; then he dropped it to the ground and let it fly. Standing at the goal line, the referee watched as the ball sailed almost perfectly down the field and straight through the goal with room still to go.

Washington State would win the game 17-0.

What fans remained in the cold temperatures raced onto the field, not just excited for what they had just witnessed, but because sports writers had declared that a victory would give the team the Northwest Conference title. Durham couldn't stop smiling about the drop kick. It was something he had always wondered whether he could accomplish. Playing for Dietz gave him the confidence to reach out past his limitations.

Coach Dietz soon had a crowd gathering around him—not fans, but reporters who were eager to record his comments for their papers. "Coach Dietz," said the reporter visiting from Seattle, "your team is now being hailed as the champions of the Northwest; any comment on that?" Dietz replied, "I am happy for that distinction. This team of men has truly withstood the best competition possible."

"But Coach," said the local Pullman reporter, "your record is the same as the University of Washington. And they beat Whitman by a score of 27-0. Does that mean Washington should be the champion?"

"Not so fast," perked up Dietz. "It would be unfair to consider today's icy conditions to be a just comparison by any standard." But Dietz didn't stop there, adding, "I have seen Washington play, and I am here to tell you they would have a difficult time stopping these men from Washington State." Coaches rarely speak out against each other, but Dietz had been planning his words very carefully. "I will tell you how to beat them. Clearly, anyone who can solve the 'off-tackle' play of Hap Miller has solved Dobie's offense."

Dietz was talking about the running skills of Miller, the Washington running back, often mentioned for national honors alongside Washington State's Bangs. But Dietz was on a roll. "Why, I am convinced my men here would 'pile the points' on Washington." The reporters were furiously writing in their pads. These comments would be fodder for many articles yet to come. Yet Dietz had one more surprise for the writers.

"To answer your question about the Northwest Championship, I believe this is the kind of question that requires an answer to be found on the field," said Dietz, offering his challenge. "Should Colorado not be able to travel to Seattle to play Washington, we would be more than happy to serve as their replacement on Thanksgiving Day." With that, Coach Dietz thanked the reporters and walked back to be with his team.

Not only had Dietz called out his rivals to the West; he had now formally challenged Coach Dobie and his team to a contest in just two weeks.

Rose Bowl

When it came down to reputation, the University of Washington stood out as a strong choice on the West Coast. Under Head Coach Gil Dobie, the UW team had not lost a single game, amassing a record to that point of 50-0-2.

Yet this season, the newspapers were filled with derogatory comments from fans. At issue was the team's lack of strong opponents on its schedule. The only opponent of mild note was California, with whom the team would play not once, but twice in the same season, a schedule that Dobie himself had negotiated. Newspaper articles pointed out that the team drew fewer and fewer students, putting the season's athletic budget in jeopardy. UW students themselves threatened to vote on taking over the football scheduling for the next year, a move unpopular with their head coach.

Despite being publically called out by Dietz, Gil Dobie angrily rejected any call to play WSC on Thanksgiving Day, even when Colorado was all too eager to give up its game with tough winter storms already hampering travel.

"No," Dobie said firmly. "We will NOT be playing Washington State."

Hundreds of miles to the south, the Tournament of Roses Committee was working to find the right competitor to represent the West. Every Northwest newspaper declared Washington State College to be the undefeated champion of the Northwest Conference. For weeks, writers had hailed Washington State College as being among the best teams in the nation. Key wins over the Oregon schools were critical in their assessment, especially after OAC had traveled back to beat football powerhouse Michigan Agricultural College. After all, MAC had earlier in the season knocked off cross-state rival Michigan. Just as important to the committee may have been word that thousands of fans were now following the team to away games, with special trains being arranged for fans going to the upcoming Gonzaga game.

While several of the Northwest newspapers were getting behind the team, a New York critic had now singled the team out as being among the very best in the country. A team with an undefeated record and an excited fan base was exactly what the committee was looking for in making its decision.

Washington State College would be formally invited to play against

Brown University in its first ever East versus West championship football game on New Year's Day. The telegram would go out immediately.

> To Coach William H. Dietz,
>
> Pasadena Tournament of Roses is arranging to bill football game between eastern and western teams for New Year's Day. As chairman of the sports committee—am sure can secure invitation for Pullman. Occasion offers splendid opportunity to obtain national recognition. Expenses for squad assured. Quick action necessary. Get busy—consent to come and I will do the rest.

It was signed "W. S. Kienholz," the former Washington State coach.

Awards

As team captain, Asa Clark played a role in recommending which players were deserving of the gray "W" letter award from the college. Doc Bohler and he were busy putting together their list of players to be approved by the Athletic Committee of faculty members. Their plan was a bold one. Typically, four or five players were to be selected. This year, Clark wanted the entire team to be recognized.

But Doc Bohler wasn't convinced so easily.

If he followed Clark's plan, the coveted award would be granted to players who hadn't finished the season because of injury or to underclassmen, even freshmen. But Clark was insistent. Citing the accomplishments of players such as the young Ronald Fishback, Clark asked for seventeen players to receive the award, making every member of the team part of the elite club. With the award ceremony only two nights away, Bohler agreed to send his recommendation to the faculty committee to let it decide. Pen in hand, he began writing out his request. But it was a letter he would barely finish before news arrived that would change everything.

Acceptance

It didn't take Washington State College long to accept the invitation to represent the West Coast in this inaugural championship football game. Even the faculty, caught up in football fever, voted unanimously, so long as a worthy East Coast opponent could be found. What everyone didn't know was that Brown University had already accepted.

Contracts were quickly prepared and signed, offering twenty-two players first class train tickets and full accommodations in Pasadena. Words like "Royal treatment awaiting your team," were enough to send a shiver of excitement through the players. For most of them, it meant their first trip out of the State of Washington, not to mention the chance to be treated to such luxury.

The hardest decision would be picking which players would go.

California

The Rose Bowl invitation would not be the only earth-shattering message that week. A letter delivered to Coach Dietz would shake up this team as well. The University of California had also read the press clippings and had publically declared its interests in talking with this new coach about coming to coach its team. Leaders in California had originally wanted to offer the job to Gil Dobie after hearing he was unhappy. But on the trip north to Seattle to play Washington for the second time, California had also sent an envoy over to Pullman to see what all the excitement was about with this new Coach William Dietz.

During their stay, representatives read a newspaper article about the team that cited former player and assistant coach, Tommy Tyrer, as saying what distinguished Dietz the most was that he never raised his voice to his players while coaching: "The success of the team lies in the fact the players have been willing to listen to him and that they have carried out his instructions to the letter.

This is because we all had faith in him from the start."

So far, every report back had said the same thing. Dietz wasn't just a genius when it came to football tactics; he found ways for the men to believe in him and his unorthodox methods. It was exactly what the leaders at California believed was needed when it faced teams in the upcoming Pacific Coast league on a regular basis—a league that their rival Stanford had been pushing to create.

The team decided to send an envoy to meet secretly with Coach Dietz in Spokane. Stoud, the graduate manager of the University of California, held a private conference with Dietz at the Davenport Hotel. Unfortunately, a newspaper reporter happened to get wind of the meeting and confronted Dietz with the story. "San Francisco is a pretty nice city," said Dietz. "I guess you can draw your own conclusions." Dietz, after all, had only signed a one-year contract with Washington State. While Dietz insisted no formal offer had been made, the meeting itself spoke volumes about the University of California's commitment to landing a new coach.

Gray W

The Gray W ceremony stood among the most prestigious events of the year. Uncharacteristic from other schools' awards, the Gray W was given to select individuals who displayed character, athletic prowess, and academic achievement. It stood as a mark of distinction, a level of prestige that few were awarded. And it granted those few a lifetime of access to any college sporting event and a special place at athletic functions across the state. Exclusively the mark of senior classmen, on rare occasions, the letter was granted to underclassmen who had performed unbelievable feats on the field of competition. Tonight, the room was crowded as excitement for the football program reached a fever pitch. Students, faculty, and even fans were eager to hear details of how the men of the Washington State football team had been invited to play a championship game on New Year's Day.

But first, it was time to bestow Washington State College's greatest sports honor: The Gray "W" award, which would cement the legacy of only the best.

Doc Bohler is believed to have been the one to read the proclamation: "This year, the committee has chosen to offer seventeen new letter awards to players that have proven themselves worthy on the field of competition." Clark's efforts to lobby for the award to the entire team had worked. As the names were read off, one-by-one, Coach Dietz sat patiently at the back of the stage, smiling. This was his players' time—one they had earned. But this was a moment that had an even greater meaning for Dietz. When it was his turn, he took the podium and began the traditional set of remarks you would expect from a coach.

Dietz stood proudly alongside Bohler as the award winners, one-by-one, walked across the stage. This was a rite of passage for many of them—one that would not be easily forgotten.

But there were more memories yet to be made.

CHAPTER 7

GONZAGA

PULLMAN

November 22, 1915

An exuberant mood filled Pullman. With the wheat harvest long in the books, the prices were strong now at ninety-one cents a bushel at the Portland Terminal. But this week, all talk was on the daily happenings of the football team that had captivated the community. The front pages of the Pullman paper and the Washington State College student paper, *The Evergreen*, were filled with stories about the latest developments. Regional newspaper writers had declared Washington State to be the "Champions of the Northwest," despite a storm of protest heard from University of Washington fans. With talk of a national invitational championship game, several schools had responded with a flurry of telegrams and behind-the-scenes lobbying efforts in hopes of getting the Tournament of Roses committee to change its mind. Montana even sent its own emissary to Pasadena, only to have him help bolster the case for Washington State by declaring it was a good "three touchdowns better" than cross-state rival Washington.

But the contracts had already been signed by Washington State. A hefty advance of $3,000 had been offered to pay the team's expenses. It was a first-class opportunity for the team to stand upon the national stage. All that was needed now was a worthy opponent.

Most students would head home for the traditional Thanksgiving break. But this year, many had written back to family, insisting they stay. A special booster train had been established to take fans to Spokane. It was such a popular notion that the 400-tickets sold out within hours. And why go home? Several large pre-game parties were being planned in Spokane.

The interest in Washington State College had never been more powerful. Positive headlines filled every major regional newspaper—just the kind of publicity needed to capture the hearts of college supporters across the state. Yet news that Coach Dietz was being wooed by another university had also grabbed the spotlight. Fans were pitching in to help "save their coach." Letters began pouring into the newspapers. Supporters like R.R. Bell, a W.S.C. graduate and principal of a public school in Nevada, had started up a campaign to keep Dietz by offering half a month of his salary—twenty-five dollars.

Yet Dietz remained aloof about his plans, only smiling when asked, saying, "I'm going to wait until after the season to make any decisions." Those words carried as much weight for what they didn't say as what they did.

Resignation

Gilmour Dobie was done.

Just days earlier, University of Washington students had approved a plan giving them authority to set the football schedule for the next season. Dobie had seen it as being his job, and his alone, to schedule which teams to play and when. Students believed stronger opponents should be on the schedule, especially with the headlines filled with nothing but the achievements of rival Washington State.

Despite having one year left on his contract, Dobie announced he would formally resign at the end of the season. Immediately, speculation began about several high-profile coaching positions available. But Dobie was not interested, telling one newspaper reporter he was done with football entirely, saying he had "lost his

176

drive and does not believe he can do justice to the position." His time at Washington would officially come a few days later after the team's last game with Colorado on Thanksgiving Day.

A New Direction

Publically, Coach William Dietz had told reporters he wasn't yet happy with his team's performance. But secretly, he couldn't have been more satisfied. His biggest challenge had been the outside distractions, from the invitation to play in the Rose Bowl to the headlines about the interest from the University of California. When asked, Dietz kept to the same answer, saying he would make his decision when the season was over.

Dietz knew he needed to keep his team focused on the game ahead. Gonzaga was no slouch. Dietz and Doc Bohler had traveled to Spokane to watch them play the University of Washington. Gonzaga had kept the game close until a late touchdown would finish the contest with a score of 21-7 in favor of Washington. Dietz decided to implement an entirely new offensive scheme for the game, one that would give the team a completely different look with a new formation in the backfield. It was a throwback to an offensive scheme he had helped develop back in his Carlisle Days.

The concept, called the "deadly flower," would be as unique as it was inventive. The key was that only the running back would know where the play was going. Each of the backs had proven himself as dependable and reliable as the back for whom this play was originally designed—Jim Thorpe. The lineup would be new as well. Bangs would be there, lining up behind fullbacks Basil Doane and Carl Dietz. But with the quarterback, Bull Durham, still nursing an injury, Coach Dietz decided to put in the younger Clyde Boone as an extra blocker; The freshman, whose only playing time had been when the game was already in hand, had to smile at the news. Sadly, Doane's availability for the game was in question, while Hanley would be out because of injuries.

Adding to the creative strategy, Asa Clark would be moved over to the right side with a newcomer, "Happy" Brooks, taking his spot on the left. Both tackles would be crossing behind the center at the same time to create confusion at the line. Coach Dietz knew the secret to getting around Gonzaga was to stop its nose tackle, Laird. The program said he weighed 210 pounds, but Dietz thought he could easily go 240. With linemen pulling away, the backs would get a run into the line to fill their spots, hence the "flower" pattern. With the ball snapped back to him, Bangs would race ahead and pick the best spot to move the ball. The play was called the "deadly flower" because no one really knew which path the back would be taking.

This would be among the most complex plays the team had seen to date, with lots of moving parts. But there was wisdom in the plan. It would certainly bottle up the middle, while creating moving lanes. The question would be how fast the back could make up his mind, and how fast he could get through. Practice sessions were spent walking through the play. Coach Dietz continued his strategy of "no scrimmaging."

It would take time and plenty of attention to get this play to work. But that's what Coach Dietz was counting on—keeping his players focused on the game, instead of the distractions all around, that seemed to emerge on a nearly daily occurrence.

All-League

In past years, one of Washington State's players being named to the "All-Conference" was rare enough to be celebrated by the team. But this year, four Washington State players were listed on the starting team: Of course, there was Benton Bangs, whom many believed was a strong contender for All-American at running back; plus his counter-part Carl Dietz at fullback; the center, Alfred Langdon; and Hack Applequist at guard. Surprisingly, the team's Captain Asa Clark did not make the list. When asked, the writer said he left

Clark out because he had missed parts of games in Oregon (and Idaho). While in past years such an honor would result in a special celebration, this year just seemed different; instead, fans were eager for the next game to begin. Many were certain the biggest honors were yet to come in the national championship game.

Brown

The Tournament of Roses committee had made it publically known.

Brown University had officially accepted a bid to represent the best in the East in the New Year's Day Tournament of Roses game, ending an incessant amount of speculation and discussion. The team would travel all the way from Rhode Island to compete in the nation's first East versus West Championship.

The match-up was now set.

Fans

It was near pandemonium at the train station in Pullman as hundreds of fans descended to see their beloved team off to the game. Joining them would be a sold-out section of the train with some 400 fans who had bought tickets for this special train to Spokane. The championship game ahead was set aside in the minds of most fans. The team had one last game left to play on Thanksgiving Day. In a rare sight, the train had to load passengers and then pull forward so the conductors could load another series of passengers at this small town station.

The front car had been reserved for the team.

Cheer Captain Pug Barnes was walking up and down the aisles, engaging each car in a series of chants and songs. He promised he would personally lead a special serpentine through town, creating a long line of fans who were sure to cause pandemonium in the streets, stopping traffic and halting pedestrians as they made their way from the Spokane train station up the hill to the famous Davenport Hotel. A special reception had been set up there by alums living in town who wanted to receive the team and its fans in style. It would be the largest visiting crowd Washington State had ever brought to a game. So large that Gonzaga had added a special section of seats to accommodate all of these incoming ticket buyers.

Doc Bohler, the master tactician when it came to logistics, walked through the car, getting his players up and ready. He worried that if they didn't get off the train quickly, they would get caught up in the crowd and never even make it to the hotel.

His advice proved to be spot on.

As the train pulled into the station, over a thousand additional fans were waiting to greet the team. Many were students home from break, who had brought family with them to see these mighty warriors from Pullman. A contingency of police officers moved in quickly to help escort the players.

Jumping from the train, it didn't take Pug Barnes long to rally the fans into one long serpentine line. Between the hundreds who had gathered and the hundreds still piling off the train, the line stretched through most of the town. Afternoon traffic began to get backed up. When a few cars tried to push their way through the crowd, a number of fans rallied to give the car a good "shake"!

Not wanting to miss out on the fun, fans from nearby Gonzaga launched their own serpentine weave, creating not one, but two lines of fans weaving through the city. Eventually, both sides came together at the downtown hotel, where some went inside, but most were just happy to be outside as part of the crowd. By nightfall, many had disappeared, but those inside stayed and danced well into the evening.

Pug Barnes become so "partied" that he was last seen roaming the halls of the hotel in only his pajamas. A feat he may have been coaxed to repeat since he long stood accused of also wearing them on a train returning from Oregon. His endless energy also had him working up a number of new songs he insisted his fellow students know and practice by game time.

The fans were certainly ready.

Kick-Off

The 2 p.m. kick-off could not have come at a better time. The temperatures were warm, the air dry. The field at the popular Natatorium Park was a dramatic turnaround from the icy conditions just two weeks prior in Pullman. There were pockets of water in places, but at least the field wasn't icy. Over in the special section of seats brought in for Washington State fans, there was virtually nowhere left to sit. Many believed there were more fans here from Washington State, than there were from Gonzaga.

Whatever nervousness the team may have felt from adapting to a new offense would soon be relieved. Washington State had won the toss and elected to receive, downing the ball on the WSC 35-yard line.

Fans greeted the team with an enormous voice. The team did not disappoint. On the first snap, the brilliance of this new scheme was quickly apparent. The play gave off the appearance of sheer pandemonium, with linemen going left and right. Blockers were pushing just about everywhere. The center dove out at their large nose tackle and took his legs right out from under him. Suddenly, there he was. Benton Bangs appeared through the crowd at full speed.

One play—25 yards.

By design, Alfred Langdon would engage the large nose tackle and

181

then slip down into a shoulder roll. After all, Langdon was giving up an easy fifty pounds to this brute. On the next play, Bangs again, only this time he cut back against the grain and shot out for another 30 yards.

Hold on—the referee had flagged the play.

"Holding, on the center," came the referee's response. Not only had WSC lost the 30-yard gain, but a 10-yard penalty had been tacked on as well. No matter. The team lined up again in the "deadly flower" formation. This time, Carl Dietz drove off the right side behind Ron Fishback and shot ahead for another 25 yards.

Again, the whistle blew the play dead; another penalty—this time on Fishback.

"Holding," was the call.

"What?" asked the confused freshman.

"Can't tackle the defender," answered the referee.

Back came the ball, giving the team second down now and 30 yards to go.

"Apple-2," whispered Durham—going back to their original offense. On the snap, Bangs took the ball out of the air, racing to the edge. The crowd roared as he shot out to the right side, with virtually no one to stop him, racing 50 yards down the field before being pushed out of bounds by the back side defender.

Again, the whistle blew.

"Holding," was the call, this time on the outside end, Hanley.

The players became visibly agitated. They were using the same schemes and blocking styles they had used all year. Only this time, a new referee was penalizing them on virtually every play. The quarterback Durham regrouped, going back to the team's older play scheme.

On the next two plays, Washington State ran the ball straight forward. It didn't do too badly, but with the penalties added, the distance for a first down was just too much. It would have to punt the ball away. Over on the sidelines, the team huddled around Coach Dietz for advice.

Coach Dietz didn't quite understand the calls either. His only advice was for players to make sure their hands were kept close to their bodies to avoid another penalty. The offense didn't have much time to think. The defense had completely smothered Gonzaga. Ronald Fishback had taken his frustrations out by blasting through the line and tackling both the quarterback and the halfback for a loss. Three plays and out. Gonzaga would be punting.

On the first play, the "deadly flower" formation opened a huge hold for Benton Bangs to exploit. Forty yards down the field he scampered. Durham looked at the referee to see his reaction: no flag. The play would hold.

Calling it again as they approached the line of scrimmage, the referee could see the Gonzaga nose tackle Laird growing frustrated; the body roll by Alfred Langdon had completely frozen him in place. When a player is falling forward, his hands automatically drop to the ground—preventing him from reaching out and even slowing the runner down. The next play, Carl Dietz shot off to the right, all the way down to the Gonzaga 5-yard line.

But a whistle from the referee immediately cancelled any jubilation. "Holding" was the call, again on the center, Alfred Langdon. Langdon was usually the calmest player on the field, but his frustrations began to mount. After the team moved back to its tried and true formation, Carl Dietz blasted forward as the lead blocker, with Bangs racing to the outside as a diversion. That meant Clyde Boone would get his first carry inside. The beefy nose tackle quickly shook off the block of Langdon and smothered Boone for a short gain.

On the next play, Bangs grabbed the ball and raced toward the middle. Langdon at center engaged the nose tackle directly, then dropped down into a body roll. With Laird pushing forward, the move completely collapsed him on top of Langdon while Bangs shot off the left side untouched 40 yards for a touchdown.

The crowd from Washington State went crazy.

Again, the jubilation quickly evaporated as the referee waved his hands since a yellow flag lay on the ground. "Holding" was again the call, and once again on Alfred Langdon. Before Durham could get to his lanky center, Langdon rushed straight up into the face of the referee, unleashing a fusillade of angry words and derogatory offerings.

The referee waited patiently for Langdon to have his say, until Durham could get to him. As soon as a few Washington State players pulled their center away, the referee took off his hat and tossed it to the ground. A second penalty had been called for "unsportsmanlike conduct."

Walking over to Coach Dietz, who remained surprisingly calm, the referee announced that Langdon would be ejected. As the crowd watched in confusion, a huge roar of disapproval spread when the coach walked to the field and escorted Langdon off to the sidelines. After calming down his player, Coach Dietz turned to Doc Bohler, who again proved himself among the most resourceful of assistants with a copy of the rule book handy.

Returning back to the teams' straight up blocking scheme, Washington State slowly worked the ball down the field, ending with a quick run by Bangs up the middle, where he drove right through the clutching arms of the bigger Laird for a touchdown. Durham tried for the extra point, but missed.

Washington State had gone up 6-0 to end the first quarter.

A total of eight separate holding calls meant a loss to the team of 80 yards, plus the numerous large gains and one touchdown that had been called back. As the quarter came to an end, Coach Dietz called the referee over for a brief chat, handing him the *Spaulding's Rules of College Football* rule book that had been revised just two years before, open to the section on holding. Dietz pointed to the page that said, "using the hands by an offensive player to 'hold' an offensive player and prevent him from performing is illegal." The debate would clearly surround the use of the body that this referee had seen as holding. After all, Washington State had been using this blocking technique for five previous games without penalty.

After this last call, Dietz knew he needed to keep the pressure on the referee. Racing onto the field as the second quarter was about to begin, Dietz caught up with the ref and made sure his protests were animated enough for fans and sportswriters to take now.

Once comfortable that he had reached an agreement with the referee that his team would be allowed to use its unique blocking scheme, Dietz headed back to the sidelines. As he did so, Dietz glanced over his shoulder to see the referee reveal the decision to the opposing coach for Gonzaga. Clearly, there was no opposition to the rule discussion.

Dietz had to smile. His team's new offense was about to be unleashed.

Second Quarter

With the fear of being called for holding behind them, the offensive unit for Washington State quickly demonstrated how dominant it had become. Benton Bangs, Carl Dietz, and the newcomer, Boone, each blasted huge gains. As soon as the play was over, they popped right back up and into the next play.

Six plays, using only two-and-a-half minutes, and Washington State would score again, giving it a 13-0 lead.

While the offense captured most of Coach Dietz's attention, it was Doc Bohler and Tommy Tyrer's defense that really took the limelight. Racing in with fresh players, the defense completely confused, penetrated, and collapsed the Gonzaga defense.

The half would end, Washington State leading Gonzaga 13-0.

Not lost on the coaches or players was the score of the University of Washington game. Washington State would need another fourteen or more points to secure bragging rights against its cross-state rivals.

Second Half

The second half would be Washington State's most remarkable half of the season. Every play on offense would easily go for 20 to 30 yards. On defense, Gonzaga could never get moving. Washington State had amassed over 300 yards in the third quarter alone, tacking on another seventeen points with two quick touchdowns and a field goal. The team had become so efficient at calling plays on the fly that it took under one minute per play for it to snap the ball, complete the play, and be ready to start the very next one.

Once Dietz had a comfortable lead, he began substituting in

players. His team had suffered several key injuries this season, so he knew how important it was to have reserves. Giving the younger players time on the field would also help build his team up for next season. The only two players he kept in the game were Durham and Clark. Durham, because he had not seen as much playing time as he had wanted in the previous few weeks, and Clark, because Dietz knew he would have a fight on his hands trying to get him to take a break.

Later when asked by a reporter, Tommy Tyrer answered, "I think it goes back to how this all got started. From the first day Dietz treated these guys like equals. He leads best by example. And this system he brought in, it's revolutionary."

True to that word, it didn't seem to matter whom Dietz put in to play. The offensive machine just kept rolling. In the final quarter, two more touchdowns and two more field goals were made by Durham.

"Zimmerman!" Coach Dietz called out. By now the starting players had begun to relax and play around behind the scenes as freshmen and sophomores were given to do most of the playing time. Speaking loud enough for everyone to hear, Dietz said, "Do you remember back in camp when someone decided to hide my pots and pans?"

Zimmerman was caught; he smiled, not knowing how else to react.

"I am certain I know who that culprit is, and it's time I did something about it," said Dietz. His words now had the rest of the team gathering around to see where the coach was going with all this.

"Zimmerman, get back to work," said Dietz. "Grab your helmet and go in for Boone." As Clarence Zimmerman raced around to find his equipment, Dietz followed right behind, almost mocking him with his tone, saying, "No good deed goes unpunished, Mr. Zimmerman. Go tell Durham you're in at running back. It's time for you to carry the ball, as much as you portend to carry this team."

As Zimmerman raced into the backfield, Durham had to glance over to the sidelines to see whether what Zimmerman was saying was actually true. From the sidelines, Coach Dietz nodded with a smile.

On first down, on the Gonzaga goal line, Zimmerman was handed the ball. The fiery redhead was suddenly reborn, slamming into the line and all but carrying three players with him into the end zone.

Zimmerman came out of the pile—up with the ball that he didn't seem to want to let go of. It would be the last touchdown of the regular season for this team, and his moment to shine. Durham's extra point would set the final score.

Washington State 40, Gonzaga 0.

The pundits certainly had their proof that Washington State was indeed the better team over the University of Washington. Given that Dobie's eleven had only beaten Gonzaga by fourteen points, even the most disbelieving writers would now be in Washington State's court. As the game ended, the Washington State players all wandered over to the sidelines to be with the fans that had come so far with them on this journey.

It would take hours for the players and fans to make their way to the train station to head back to Pullman. It seemed that no one wanted the season to end.

The good news was that one more contest was yet to be played.

Pullman

The weeks following the Gonzaga game had an almost surreal feeling. Dietz had cancelled all practices for the next ten days. Players, who had become used to a set schedule, found themselves with afternoons and weekends off. Coach Dietz himself had volunteered to lead a team of faculty members in a grudge match of a basketball game for a team calling itself the "Lone Stars."

The life of a student-athlete is an intense mixture of two lives into one. Each must find a way to be both a full-time student and a full-time athlete, a difficult task for anyone to squeeze into one life, let alone into the life of a young person just starting adulthood. Yet it is within these formative years that friendships and relationships are forged that will remain tightly bound for a lifetime.

As the school year headed into the holidays, it was customary for couples to consider matrimony, many often becoming engaged just before Christmas. Thoughts of the future likely filled the minds of Lillian McDonald and Helen Quarrels. While it was true that some women came to college with hopes of finding a husband, such was not the case with Lillian. She had come here to be a teacher, a profession that has loosened its boundaries in recent years to allow instructors to marry, yet there remained an unspoken tradition that asked women to dedicate their lives to the teaching of young minds, and not to children of their own.

That was until Asa Clark showed up. Lillian's life had been full as a leader in the Women's League on campus, a member of the Women's Athletic Club, and a volunteer at the YWCA. Her strong grades had given her a choice of several teaching opportunities, and she had been talking with educators in Cheney, Washington, near her hometown of Spokane, about a position after her graduation.

But college has a way of shaping, even changing, a person's life. In Lillian's case, her life had been completely turned upside down.

Logistics

Doc Bohler lived and breathed logistics. He thrived on them. For him, logistics was about making connections that created an amazing experience. The negotiations with Pasadena had been difficult. Organizers couldn't understand why Washington State needed so many players. The team's initial request for twenty-eight players had been flatly rejected. The team could only travel with sixteen players and two coaches.

While Bohler tried to figure out this conundrum, President Bryan offered to pay for the university's top money man, William Kruegel, to go with the team and be in charge of finances. Kruegel was a great choice since he also served on the college's Athletic Committee and had helped find resources for the team all season.

There were the expected hiccups.

Charlotte Kruegel became quite upset when she learned her husband would not be home for Christmas. The level-headed William made peace by agreeing to take both her and their two young children along, even paying their way.

Meanwhile, the tournament committee remained adamant about the number of players it would allow because it didn't want to imply it was playing favorites by offering to pay for more players than it was for Brown University, which was traveling a considerably longer distance. In the end, Bohler negotiated to bring their players, two coaches, graduate students, and a trainer. He himself was listed as the official "trainer." In truth, the graduate students would be players. Bohler dropped his pen to his desk and sat back in relief. He had finagled a way to take twenty players to the Rose Bowl. It would be up to Coach Dietz to determine just whom they would be.

It was a hectic time. While Bohler was busy trying to line up the logistics for this trip, a constant barrage of letters and telegrams continued to arrive. One of particular note was Oregon's Agricultural

College's coach, asking for a rematch this season. Bohler only shook his head.

What should have been a routine exercise in transportation and lodging had blossomed into this enormously complicated trip, as alumni groups up and down the coast all wanted to host a special event. Not only that, the Tournament of Roses committee had set up a variety of tourist destinations for the team, with the implication that with several donors to this big game in attendance, the presence of the team would be expected.

Hollywood

Tom Brown was one of the most popular fictional characters of the day. His exploits had long entertained people across the country through a series of stories and plays. Each carried a consistent theme of love won through adversary. The story often surrounded Tom, a young man who undergoes a series of trials and mistakes to gain the attention of a young woman.

In Hollywood, as filmmaking began to prosper, studios often turned to well-tested Broadway shows and popular storylines in hopes of attracting a built-in audience. William Selig was among the founding pioneers who fell in love with the film business. A vaudeville performer and a magician by training, the young Selig had formed the very first motion-picture studio in Hollywood.

As he read the paper one December morning, one name jumped to his attention. William "Lone Star" Dietz would be coming to Pasadena with his football team to play in the biggest game in modern history. Selig shook his head. Dietz and he shared a history going back nearly ten years. Dietz, while at the Carlisle School, had written to Selig, challenging the way American Indians were portrayed in the movies of the day. In Dietz's mind, Native Americans were too often portrayed as "attacking savages" or were used to create a sense of terror for the heroes of the day making their way West. "Why, native women never even wear feathers in their hair," wrote Dietz as he challenged the very vision filmmakers often adapted in their storytelling.

Selig had listened and engaged in a series of letters with Dietz that would lead to changes in the way his studio handled stories of the old West. With Dietz coming to Hollywood with a football team, Selig had an idea. His latest installment of his most popular series was getting ready to shoot *Tom Brown Goes to Harvard*. In this latest episode, his now collegiate Tom would fight for the attention of the beautiful starlet Evelyn on the football field. The story had called for Tom to sacrifice himself in the game in order to win over Evelyn's heart. Privately, filmmakers knew this notion was never rational, yet it was just the kind of story that viewers loved to see.

But finding and hiring two dozen actors to play the part of a well-rehearsed football team would prove expensive. Selig saw an opportunity in the making. With that, he reached out to Dietz with an offer that would save him money while making these football boys into movie stars.

Brown

It was bad enough that Brown had beaten Carlisle so badly this season. Coach Dietz's former school used an offense similar to his. But it was an afternoon letter that would cause Coach Dietz the most grief. It came from an old friend who wrote, "I do not like being the bearer of bad news, but I have witnessed firsthand that Carlisle Coach Kelly has given over his playbook to Brown, in order that they may understand better how to beat you."

Clearly, this would give the boys from Brown a distinct advantage.

Dietz knew what he must do. There would be a formal letter of complaint and an official protest lodged. But these rarely had much effect. Instead, Dietz now sat back in heavy thought, designing a new offensive scheme for his team that it would only have a few weeks to implement.

Pullman Preps

An enormous debate raged over where to host the official Rose Bowl party in downtown Pullman. Hundreds of fans were expected to come. The regional telegraph company had become involved, and it offered to send back dispatches for every part of the game. None of the local venues had enough seating. But that didn't keep owners from weighing in with their own ideas.

In the end, it was decided to host the event out of doors. A large football field would be painted on the side of the Pullman Hotel. Local restaurants, especially the ever popular "Rib Restaurant," known for having "the best meal in town by a good lick," would be catering. Tables would be brought in for guests to sit while dispatches would come in from the nearby telegram office.

Rose Bowl fever was about to take control.

Blankets

Blankets are deeply woven into the history of American Indians. They serve as a source of protection against the elements, as a source of warmth, and were often as individualized as the tribe itself.

The Sioux, for example, would gift a blanket with an intricate star pattern to recognize the stages of life and to honor the guides in life from each point of the compass. Lakota star quilts had become extremely popular because of the way they looked, but also for the way they felt, made of the softest of wools around.

And so it was with Washington State College. As the semester came to an end, each of the players was presented with a special wool blanket, complete with a unique design kept just for the team. The honor was so unique that as the players gathered for a team photograph, they insisted on being wrapped in their new blankets.

Practice

Temperatures had certainly dropped since these men had last taken to the field for practice. The semester was rapidly finishing up, with final exams only two weeks away. Nearly all of the players were on the field, even though several had been told they would not be making the trip to California. True to his form, Dietz had come up with a new series of plays for the trip, especially since word had leaked out that Brown had a copy of the old Carlisle playbook.

But Dietz had one big surprise for the team.

He announced the team would be part of a major motion picture. Each of the players would receive $100 dollars apiece. By comparison, newspaper ads were offering workers seven dollars to unload wagons—per week!

If the thought of traveling to California, in an all-expense paid trip to compete in a championship football game wasn't enough to fill these men's heads with lofty dreams, the reality of a hefty payday certainly would have only added to the fairytale nature of what was ahead.

CHAPTER 8
ROSE BOWL

PULLMAN DEPARTURE

Wednesday, December 21, 1915

The day of departure had come quickly.

As the players readied for the train headed south, the trip began to take on a surreal feeling. Pasadena was all the talk, offering sunshine and modern conveniences, where all the roads were paved and nearly everyone owned a car. The timing of the trip also meant the men would not be with their families or loved ones for Christmas. Holiday plans were now filled with promises of dances and feasts, movie stars and football—an unbelievable journey for some two dozen college students who had never imagined such was possible only three months earlier.

The weeks since Thanksgiving were a blur. As students, many players spent nights catching up on semester work, while studying for final exams. As athletes, they were learning yet another new offensive scheme Coach Dietz had implemented, while staying in shape with plenty of conditioning. Despite the break, Coach Dietz kept to his practice of allowing very little contact in the team's drills. Making the dream of California more enticing, a bitter cold snap had struck the Palouse with blowing snow and temperatures well below freezing.

Dietz himself had turned to more creative pursuits. He had agreed to help the Glee Club prepare a series of Indian songs from his youth for a special program by the club the next spring.

At the train station, both Lillian McDonald and Helen Quarrels were there to see their men off. The women were both from nearby Spokane, some seventy miles to the north, and pledged to spend time together while their boys were away. Neither had a ring on her finger, a fact that did not go unnoticed by either. Perhaps their men had just been too busy, but for whatever reason, neither Ace Clark nor Benton Bangs had proposed. Instead, the women were likely filled with questions: How would this trip change these men? Would they return unchanged? Or, their greatest fear, would this journey change the way they saw life forever?

From the beginning, the team would learn what it meant to receive the "royal treatment." Boarding the train, the players were quickly ushered toward the front to ride in a retrofitted Pullman car. Several benches had been removed to allow for greater space between seats for the athletes. New tapestries lined the walls and ceiling. Extra attendants were on hand to ensure all needs would be met. The itinerary ahead was reflective of the team's newfound celebrity status; first stop, Spokane for a special dinner, before boarding an evening train for Portland, with similar parties and events to be held in San Francisco and Southern California.

Their final stop would be in sunny California in time for Christmas.

As they settled into their seats, the players' talk likely surrounded the topics of becoming movie stars or being held up as honored guests at a series of banquets. Each day, it seemed new word came of yet another celebration or honor. Somewhere in the middle of it all, they would need to prepare for the grandest football game ever held.

Because the train rolled into Spokane late in the evening, some 200 business leaders and football fans had already begun eating when the players walked into the celebration. The lavish feast was sponsored by the local banks, which had just completed "their most successful year ever." President Bryan and the WSC Board of

Regents were already there for official meetings. In what would be Bryan's last official act as President, the Board eagerly approved a long-term building plan for the campus that would add four major science and agriculture facilities, while adapting a quadrangle design for the campus, clearly ignoring any threat their science programs would be shut down.

Coach Dietz seemed like the only one in the room not assured of victory. "I predict a hard battle and promise to have the men decorated in full 'war paint' when the whistle blows to start the contest," proclaimed Dietz when asked to say a few words.

There would be no pause for the team that evening. As soon as the meal was complete, Doc Bohler herded the team quickly to the train headed for Portland. It was well after midnight when the players stumbled into their hotel for the night.

Coach Dietz had scheduled a series of workouts along the way. With the warmer temperatures in Portland, he bowed to his players wishes to allow scrimmaging. But after the fullback, Doane, twisted his knee and the younger Herreid broke his nose, all scrimmages on the trip would be cancelled. Still, Dietz worried that his team wasn't ready, so he scheduled another workout in San Francisco the following day. Those plans were dashed when the train south was delayed. The delay also caused a brief panic among the train workers who realized they didn't have provisions for either breakfast or lunch. But after two nights of heavy eating, few players even seemed to notice.

In the background of the trip was talk of Coach Dietz staying on at Washington State. The University of Nebraska had now entered the picture, offering Dietz a head coaching job. The University of California was eager to talk with the coach as well. Strong efforts were made to come up with a better salary at Washington State. Doc Bohler had been in talks with his regents and the president to make Dietz a handsome offer, but Dietz immediately dismissed any discussion, saying he would make his decision after the game, a pronouncement that worried Bohler and others that Dietz was not likely staying around.

San Francisco

In San Francisco, Washington State alums had put together a full day of events. Onboard the train, the Shasta Limited, there was some excitement when Doc Bohler announced he had booked them a stay at the "world famous Baghdad by the Bay hotel." It promised to be an evening filled with even more elegance and extravagance than the night before.

Meeting the team first thing in the morning, the alums took the players on an automobile tour of the city, complete with visits to the Golden Gate Bridge and the Presidio. A surprise guest, Gil Dobie, joined the tour and stuck around for the team's practice. He spent time talking with Coach Dietz, wishing the coach all the best. After practice, the team indulged in a special saltwater bath, compliments of the Olympic Club.

Headlines in the newspaper that day were filled with war atrocities. Already, Britain had lost over half-a-million men in the conflict. But for these players, the talk of war was temporarily set aside.

They had their own battle just ahead.

Christmas Morning in California

At each stop, the fans and admirers seemed to step things up another notch. A lavish feast prepared in San Francisco had many of the travelers nearly missing the morning train to Los Angeles. Each had overeaten, overindulged, and overexposed himself to the growing numbers of fans eager to meet the team the press called the battling "warriors." Newspaper men seemed to be waiting at every door. And a new type of fan began to emerge—young women, each one eager to make the men's acquaintance.

As the train pulled into the Los Angeles train station, a brass band fired up the Washington State fight song. Piling off the train, the men were greeted by the Tournament of Roses committee. Fans had lined up along the railing to see these athletes from the north. Adding to the surreal atmosphere, film crews captured every moment. The studio crew was said to need the footage in its upcoming film. For A.J. Bertonneau and the rest of the committee, the arrival was as much a celebration as it was a designed performance. Months of campaigning with reporters and newspaper owners had generated an enormous amount of publicity for the big game.

If the trappings along the way had spoiled the players' senses, then the offerings of Pasadena were purely opulent. The city itself was a modern marvel, rich with every convenience, including electric trolleys running down five-lane roads. Motor cars of all shapes and sizes passed through the streets. It was an enclave of delight for two dozen simple travelers from a small town up north. At the small train station in the center of town, hundreds of fans had lined up to greet the team—"warriors from the North" as the papers had begun to describe them. Pasadena was the mecca of entertainment for much of the world. Traveling vaudeville shows and circus performers would settle here to work and train during the harsh winter months before giving performances all over the world. The movie business had kicked off into full swing, attracting entertainers and would-be starlets from across the land.

Few of the players even realized it was Christmas Day.

Five large motor cars, with soft convertible tops, brought them to the front of the hotel, where uniformed attendants raced to open the doors to usher them inside. The drivers would be at the players' disposal for their entire visit.

"Welcome to the Hotel Maryland, gentlemen," said the booming voice of the bell captain. As players went to their grab suitcases, they were cut off by bellmen under strict rules that no guest would touch his own bag. Ushered into the main lobby of the hotel, the team was met by an impeccably-tailored gentleman who waited patiently for their arrival. As they walked toward the front desk, the scenery around the team was almost too much to take in at one blush. Intricate designs were woven into even the most simple of trims and tapestries. Beautiful paintings, some looking like those found in art galleries, were tastefully displayed with just the right splash of light to enhance their features. But perhaps the biggest surprise was the other guests passing by; to them, all this beauty seemed invisible. Instead of looking out, their faces were staring in toward the team. Not lost on the team were the admiring glances and inviting smiles of a number of simply beautiful young women, eager to return a glance with a "Hello" or "Good afternoon." The team was settled in with the promise of a special Christmas Dinner, along with a full schedule the next day. For the tournament committee, this was all part of its master plan. The team had been publically promised that every need and whim would be taken care of during its visit.

What team in the future wouldn't want to enjoy similar treatment?

Distances

Lillian McDonald's thoughts were far from the typical family holidays filled with food and family. Her mind was likely several thousand miles away, thinking of the brawny man who had changed everything in her life. Lillian had long prided herself on being fiercely independent.

Her friend, Helen Quarrels, stopped by with a stack of newspapers for the pair to read up on the adventures their two favorite men were enjoying. Even though the couples were separated by time and distance, these articles brought their actions to life as if they were happening in the moment.

From the first headlines, it was clear this was far more than a football trip. Writers were caught up in capturing nearly every minute of the trip south. "From the minute of their arrival in Pasadena the football men were idolized," read the newspaper. "The first evening was marked with a dance in the Hotel Maryland in their honor."

The team had long since arrived by the time the story was published. "The following day they journeyed to the automobile races at Ascot Park. At the Maryland hotel special automobiles were retained at the door constantly for the services of the distinguished guests." The women must have read these glamorous stories with some level of concern. Would their men want to come back to their ordinary lives after such treatment?

Pasadena

A rather quiet group of men ambled their way to waiting cars for a day of local sightseeing. The dinner the evening before had turned into an elaborate party, with the band playing late, an endless supply of dance partners, and something to which these men were not accustomed—alcohol. Unlike in Pullman, there were no rules in Pasadena against drinking. At one point, Mrs. Bohler, who had accompanied her husband on the trip, had grown upset, choosing to return to her room rather than bear witness to the evening's frivolities.

Now on their sightseeing tour, the men were paying the price for their overnight indulgences. The first stop would be to watch a special auto race being held in their honor. Some of the top drivers of the day—Barney Oldfield, Eddie Pullen, and Dave Lewis—had all been brought in for the team's entertainment.

Spokane

Lillian and Helen were reading now from a Los Angeles paper: "The party made the trip up stately Mt. Low, as they journeyed to the magnificent Busch gardens, where they inspected the Ostrich farms." Adding, "Later the team took in 'Universal City', there to be surrounded and hailed admiringly by all the famous 'movie' people."

Surrounded by movie stars? Lavish parties?

What woman wouldn't be concerned?

Encounters

It was awkward enough that everywhere the team went, a movie crew with a camera was recording the event. Many on the team were still laughing that they had convinced Mrs. Bohler to jump into a buggy hitched up to an ostrich. The tour of Universal City was the last stop before the team headed back for yet another banquet. This time, the Downtown Business Association had sponsored a special seafood dinner. What the team didn't expect was that here in the land of actors and filmmakers, the Washington State players would find themselves held up as the true celebrities.

Once they arrived at the film studio, Coach Dietz disappeared, leaving the team to wander with a single tour guide around the numerous buildings and sets. Actors were walking around in various costumes. Workers were pushing large lights or putting up riggings. It was a glimpse behind the curtain of an industry these men had only known from the finished product down at the cinema on that rare occasion when they could come up with the five cents needed for admission.

The tour guide, a young man in his twenties, was giving the men a cursory view of the studio, pausing to let them watch an outdoor scene being filmed. It was a simple one, where a pair of riders on horseback went past the camera. The background was a Western town that only seemed to have the fronts of the buildings, and nothing out back.

It was fascinating work to watch.

The tour would be interrupted by a beautiful young woman named Hazel Daly. As the men admired her light hair and bright blue eyes, she extended out her long thin arms to shake hands. Whatever flirtations she delivered were quickly dashed by a handsomely dressed man named Harry Beaumont, who introduced himself as the director of the film the team would be working on the next week. Hazel would be the leading lady.

Hazel may have gone out of her way to appear single and available. The newspapers loved to print out gossip. There was a hint that Hazel may have had her eye on someone on the team. But in truth, her director Harry and she had been carrying on a secret relationship for some time.

Spokane

Back in Spokane, Helen and Lillian met regularly, with the day's newspaper articles being their main topic of conversation.

"At their hotel the players were masters of all they saw," the stories read. "Dances, dinners and receptions in their honor followed in rapid succession until Coach Dietz, fearful of the effects on the warriors, cut down materially on their social rations."

No amount of worrying would help ease any concerns here. Both women would have to wait until their men returned. Only the chance to look directly into their men's eyes for the truth might relieve them, depending on what those eyes would reveal.

Practice

Washington State's first day of practice proved to be a disaster.

The handful of men who showed up in the lobby were in no shape to begin training. Another late night of dancing, feasting, and yes, drinking had left the team completely wiped out. Coach Dietz looked at his players, realizing there would be no football practice this day. Even worse, there were still a number of evening events left on the team's schedule. Both Bohler and he had to wonder just how much overindulgence one team could manage. Dietz would cancel practice and ask Bohler to cancel several upcoming events as politely as possible.

The team was set to begin filming early the next morning. Dietz was hoping it might get in some practice between takes.

Movie Making

It doesn't take long for the glamour of movie making to wear off.

What the players quickly learned was that most of the time is spent getting things ready for each shot. Lights needed to be set up; rehearsals were held with the actors for where to stand and when to speak; even setting up the camera seemed to take forever. The other roughly 10 percent of the time was spent doing the same scene, over and over again, until the director was satisfied with his shot.

Much of the script called for the team to be in the background practicing. For the players from Washington State, it was difficult to follow along with the storyline. Crews would often shoot different scenes for the movie in the exact same location. Nothing seemed to be in the right order. At the same time, Coach Dietz was trying to get them to master the offensive scheme they had adapted a few weeks before.

The scheme was an idea Dietz had developed during the game against Gonzaga. His team had become exceptionally adept at running plays, one right after another. Even Dietz himself was surprised to learn his offense had mustered 135 offensive plays against Gonzaga, a record for a single game. Dietz knew the advantage this could give his team.

The new concept was a simple one. Instead of calling a play in advance, his quarterback would signal where to run almost entirely at the line of scrimmage after he saw how the defense was set. The real advantage was in the backfield. His quarterback, Durham, had developed a simple hand signal for his backs that let them silently know who would be getting the ball. Blockers up front were only told whether the play would be going to the left, center, right, or if it was a passing play. The key was to keep drilling the players over and over again until this new concept became second nature.

With the movie schedule, players needed to be on the field drilling continuously from 8 a.m. until a lunch break and then back at it until the sun began to fall. Not surprisingly, some of the players began to grumble.

For both Clarence Zimmerman and Hack Applequist, the long days led them to believe they had been tricked by Dietz into excess practicing. The two had seen a copy of the movie script and saw that the final scene called for the star of the movie to burst over the line for a winning touchdown. On several occasions, they could be seen huddling together as if to form some conspiracy.

During this time frame, an intriguing concept came forward. Brown had become the heavy favorite at local gambling houses, with odds as high as three-to-one odds. Players began contemplating using their earnings from the movie to bet on themselves. Heading home with $300 in their pockets would add yet another surreal layer to the trip.

Strategy

Across town, Brown University was hosting its own practice sessions. The team had not yet closed its practices, giving Dietz and Bohler an idea. The pair decided to sneak a peek at their opponents, especially at the centerpiece to the team—Fritz Pollard. With an enormous chest and thin waist, this 260-pound runner moved so low and so fast down the field that the papers called him "the torpedo." Writers said they had witnessed how four or five opponents were needed to bring him down. Pollard was the first African-American to play in the upper ranks of college football. Talk was he had once run for 300 yards in a single game.

The player whom Coach Dietz and Doc Bohler saw was truly an impressive sight. Even in practice, Pollard was difficult to stop. He was the ultimate football player—not only fast, but able to change directions quickly and then power his way forward.

After watching quietly, Dietz had seen enough. As Bohler and he headed back to the hotel, the normally talkative Dietz did not say a single word.

A Wrap

It would be the final scene of the movie, and Director Harry Beaumont wanted it to be grand. "Tom" needed to score a touchdown in an impressive enough fashion that he would win over the heart of his true love. The entire movie had been shot except for this scene, and Beaumont insisted this would be the film's defining moment.

Clarence Zimmerman and Hack Applequist had a plan. They offered to give Tom a real fight at the line of scrimmage, and then allow him to jump over the two into the end zone. It was just what Beaumont wanted. The rest of the players were a bit surprised at the gracious offer. Both Hack and Zimmerman were suddenly excited, even patting themselves on the back. Several players began to suspect something was up.

For the next hour, the camera focused on the backfield with the star getting the handoff and running straight into the line. The final shot was set-up in the end zone. Tom, both his real name and the name of his character, would fight through the line and jump into the end zone right in front of the camera, his arms raised triumphantly. But the crew felt the pressure to move things quickly. It was the last day of shooting and the sun had begun to set.

Fans were positioned into the stands in the background. The camera was set, the actors in place, the scene ready to roll.

As the director called out "Action," the quarterback spun around and handed the ball off to Tom, who raced straight toward the camera as the hole in the line appeared to open up. Suddenly, both Zimmerman and Applequist dropped their shoulders in front of the actor. In the collision, Tom fought to get through when the pair suddenly raised up, tossing the actor head over heels into the air.

In almost slow motion, Tom did a complete flip as he sailed several feet high, then landed with a thud loud enough to be heard across the way. But Tom jumped up, raising the football while looking into the camera with a true look of triumph on his face.

"Perfect!" said the director, as he walked over to congratulate both of the Washington State men for their role. The shot became the signature scene of the film. Beaumont began shaking hands with the team, knowing he had a real winner in the can. Glancing over, he noticed his star begin to stagger. Without warning, Tom Moore collapsed to the ground. Rushing to his side, Beaumont saw that Moore appeared to be O.K., but a trip to the doctor would be needed to be sure.

With the very last movie scene complete, it was now time for the team to focus its attentions on one last football game on New Year's Day.

New Year's Eve

December 31, 1915

Pasadena, California

Electricity in the air surrounded Pasadena as thousands of visitors made their way to the annual festival the next day. Coach Dietz had relented and allowed the Washington State football coaches and players to celebrate New Year's Eve. Tournament hosts had gently applied some pressure for them to attend, especially since the team had canceled several events the past week due to Coach Dietz's fear of "overindulgence."

As the meal wrapped up, Dietz asked Bohler to get everyone's attention. Clinking his glass with his knife, Bohler quickly silenced the room as Dietz rose to speak. The coach thanked his players for a tremendous season and asked them to turn in as early as they could. After all, the game would be played the following day.

Tonight, William Dietz was not himself. Often as flamboyant as he dressed, Dietz was noticeably quiet. Wrapping up his words, Dietz turned away, saying he was heading to his room. Doc Bohler watched closely. While he hadn't known Dietz long, he knew enough to know that his head coach was deeply troubled.

Trouble

It took several knocks before Dietz finally said, "Come in—it's open."

Doc Bohler walked in to find Dietz sitting at his parlor table. A glass of what looked like Scotch was sitting beside him. Odd, because it was the first drink Bohler had ever seen Dietz have. On closer look, he realized the drink had not been touched.

Bohler waited patiently for Dietz to speak. After a long pause, Dietz turned to him with a sad, yet honest voice, saying, "It's Pollard." Looking away, Dietz was clearly troubled, like a man used to having answers and suddenly having none. Dietz told Bohler there would be no way his team could win the next day. Pollard was just too much of a force for his lightweight team to overcome.

The two sat in a long, quiet silence.

It didn't seem right, that this team had come so far to feel beaten before it even took the field. But Bohler knew that if Dietz didn't have an answer, then no one did. Eventually, Bohler stood to leave, heading off to his own room. There wasn't much point in celebrating now. One last glance back saw Dietz lay down on his bed without undressing, just staring at the ceiling.

There would be little sleep for either man this night.

Shortly before Dietz had left the Carlisle Indian School for Pullman, he had shared with his teammate Alex Arcasa that he had a premonition he would rise to stardom and achieve greatness only to suffer a tremendous fall, even comparing himself to Mozart, who died at age thirty-five and was buried in a pauper's grave. After seeing Pollard for himself, Dietz had also confided in a newspaper reporter that he didn't believe his team could win.

Dietz had to suffer at the wonder of it all, reflecting on how far they had come, only to realize greatness would not be theirs to hold.

Revelations

Dietz was in somewhat of a foggy haze when he slowly woke, realizing there was a violent pounding on the door. Slow in coming to his senses, he unlocked the door only to have Bohler burst inside.

An excited Bohler grabbed Dietz by the arm and dragged him over to the window. Pulling the curtain aside, he motioned for Dietz to look out. Groggily, Dietz looked, but he couldn't understand what Bohler was so excited about.

It's raining!" pronounced Bohler.

Dietz looked out again.

"No, I mean it's *really* raining," said Bohler excitedly.

Dietz looked at Bohler confused.

"Don't you see," said Bohler. "This rain will make everything muddy. Pollard can't get any traction in this!"

Dietz's eyes shot open. There just might be a way to stop Pollard, and with him, Brown. Excitedly looking for his belongings, Dietz turned to Bohler and said, "Get the team together. We have work to do!"

211

Pullman

There is something about sports that has the power to unite. People from all walks of life, of differing religions, even of varied politics, all set aside differences to share in the glory of the game. The only acceptance needed is to look at your fellow fan and know that he is one with you.

A light coating of snow had fallen on the Palouse region that surrounded the town of Pullman. It was quiet now, but preparations had been ongoing for days for today's big event.

A large football field had been painted on the side of the pharmacy, next to the hotel. Already, the hickory wood was cooking up meats from the local rib shop for the festival. Despite the campus being mostly empty, hundreds of football fans were expected to be on hand for today's big event. A paper football had been mounted on a long pole to be moved back and forth along the gridiron on the wall as updates came in. A large blackboard had been brought down from the school in order to write out the score. Dispatches were promised via telegram from Pasadena. For the first time, a Pullman team playing over one-thousand miles away would offer immediate results to its fans. The game itself wasn't set to begin until 2 p.m., but eager fans had begun to wander downtown where telegram dispatches would be received to keep everyone up-to-date.

The game, it seems, was about to begin.

The Rose Bowl

Outside the hotel, the sounds of marching bands echoed through the buildings. A continuous line of floats glided past covered with thousands of flowers, each attached by hand. Several of the newer ones glided on the frames of automobiles, while others were pulled by an amazing array of matching horses. For the people of Pasadena, this was the true reason to celebrate. The football game was merely a way of bringing more national attention to this popular festival. Yet the Washington State football team would be late to the parade. It was huddled into a corner of the hotel restaurant, making plans for how to stop Brown, especially its powerful running back Pollard.

Dietz knew his team needed to get to Pollard early. With the wet conditions, the large back wouldn't be able to get outside easily. Changing the defensive set, Dietz would add two ends to the defensive line. The linebackers would be up close as well. The entire goal was to force everything inside and get as many bodies as possible to push Pollard back. The biggest threat would be if Brown decided to pass. With all of the defenders cheating close, a pass threatened to beat them deep.

On the offense, Dietz decided to add in some of the same trickery the defense had deployed all season. The offensive linemen would be allowed to move around and not get set until just before the ball was snapped. That way, they could get an advantage by choosing how to line up against the defenders. Using a modified version of the "deadly flower" strategy, the plan was for blockers just to push forward while the running back looked for the best hole on the run.

It wouldn't be pretty. But it might be the only way to move the ball on a day like this.

Players were interrupted by Doc Bohler, who had just appeared holding a large box. Bohler had a large grin on his face. No one should have been surprised given Doc's ability to scrounge for what the team needed. Opening the box, Bohler pulled out several dozen new football shoes. All of them were made out of leather, with each shoe containing one critical difference. Long spikes, nearly two inches in length, adorned each.

Smiling, Bohler said, "They're mud spikes."

That grin was infectious. Dietz himself began to smile. He began to believe they might just win this game.

In all the new excitement, Dietz made a bold proclamation: "I have decided to put my fate in your hands." Standing, Dietz declared, "If you beat Brown this day…then I will guarantee I will return to be your coach next season."

Many in the room looked at each other with excited grins. These were the words they had longed to hear.

Premonitions

From the moment Carl Dietz woke up, he had a premonition that the weight of this day would be upon him. As he listened to the coach outlining his new scheme, he understood why. This strategy would require someone to push his way through the line, using whatever small opening might appear.

Carl Dietz was just that type of player.

In the annuals of time, great burdens have been placed on individuals who faced tremendous odds. Yet if you asked them what thought went through their minds at the moment of discovery, many would all say the exact same thing, "I just knew." And so it was for Carl Dietz. He tried to make a mental checklist of his emotions and realized the only thing he carried was a sense of "certainty."

Life had seemed so much simpler just a few short months ago.

A small town boy from Bremerton, Washington, Carl Dietz had come to Washington State to learn how to be an electrical engineer. His plan was to return home and excel at the Naval shipyards there that had fed his family for years. But the journey home had taken them south to compete in the nation's first national championship football game. Taking a deep breath, he picked up his bag of football gear and headed down to be with the team.

If this were to be his day—then he was eager for it to begin.

Game Time

The heavy rains were hurting attendance for this first championship Tournament of Roses game. Seven thousand tickets had been sold, but it was far fewer than what organizers had hoped for. The committee began talking about cancelling. There was a backup plan, not shared publically. If the weather became too miserable, they would cancel the event and host it two days later on January 3rd. The idea being that fans who had traveled across the country would still stay.

Warmups

Dietz looked out at the field and tried his best to gauge its conditions. A local polo club had hosted a tournament on the field earlier that morning when the rain had come down the hardest. Heavy pockets of water had formed where hooves had dug into the soil. Right now, a marching band contest was wrapping up, involving four teams, all taking turns competing by running formations up and down the field. As he padded back and forth carrying his signature walking cane, Dietz appeared to onlookers to be pacing across the field. In reality, he walked around, pressing his cane to test the ground's firmness. On the field, he saw opportunity. In some places, large puddles had formed; in others, mud had grown thick from all the morning's wear.

But as the marching contest began to wind down, Dietz was surprised to see the fans starting to file out of the stadium. Dietz's eyes shot open; he turned to Bohler, worried the fans would believe the game cancelled. Quickly, he had Bohler rally the team onto the field. Bohler raced into the locker room to rush the players out. Many were still lacing up shoes and padding jerseys, arriving only as the last band member left the field. Jumping into their pre-game routine, Washington State began chanting and doing jumping jacks. The move left a number of fans bewildered. It was a tradition in Southern California to postpone any contest until the weather was more favorable.

The move worked.

Almost in unison, the fans turned around and headed back to their seats, not wanting to miss the opening kick-off.

Pullman

Back in Pullman, Rose Bowl fever had reached epidemic proportions. With the first telegram dispatches arriving from Pasadena, the expected crowd of 500 had already grown to three times that size. When the rib house filled up, two other businesses opened their doors with the promise of live updates via telegram.

A notably excited mood filled the crowd. In recent weeks, the number of people requesting "Old Crow" medicine, something that seemed to become more popular with the approach of each football game, had markedly increased, and this event was proving to be one of the largest.

Kick-Off

As Brown wandered out on to the field, it was clear none of the players had been in the weather very long, a sharp contrast to the team from Washington State warming up in the rain. The WSC uniforms were clinging to the players' sides. Doc Bohler had brought spare uniforms, and he had set up a system for at least wringing out the excess water to "swap-out" them for dry ones.

Brown had won the toss and elected to receive. Washington State's defense would be put immediately to the test.

The weather did not dampen the crowd's spirits. Several dozen Washington State fans had made their way south for the game and were seated in a special section behind the WSC players' bench.

The bleachers made of steel poles and wood would provide no relief from the weather. But the storm didn't deter the fans from being loud and vocal. The surrounding California hills were not enough to stop storm clouds from rolling in from the Pacific Ocean. Besides, for fans used to fighting the cold weather of Pullman, the warm rains of Southern California were almost a welcome relief.

Carl Dietz, who had proven himself a solid kicker in the harshest of weather, blasted the ball down to the Brown 15-yard line. Harold "Buzz" Andrews, the captain of the Brown team, deftly grabbed the ball and raced it back to the 30-yard line.

Brown took the field with a swagger of confidence. Outweighing the Washington State line by at least twenty pounds a man, the linemen almost sauntered into position. The center, Ken Sprague, looked left and then right and said, "Did your football team forget to make the trip?" The rest of the Brown line broke into a laugh. But no one on the Washington State team spoke. They were all keyed up and eager to burn off their early jitters.

Off the left side of the line, the big fullback, Fritz Pollard, came smashing through as a blocker. Washington State's Ronald Fishback anticipated the move, sliding away from his man and driving head-first into Pollard, who was heard to let out a groan at the hit. The move clogged up the gap, giving the rest of Washington State's team a chance to grab the halfback, Andrews, for a 1-yard gain. A simple play, but one that gave Washington State a huge amount of confidence. It had met the enemy, and it had not faltered.

With the rains pouring down, Brown decided to try its hand on defense and punt the ball on second down. Carl Dietz had convinced the coach that he be the one for punt duty. Catching the ball on the 30-yard line, he was cut down immediately by the Brown rush.

On the sideline, Coach Dietz decided that two could play that game. On first down, Washington State would answer back with its own punting contest.

Carl Dietz grabbed the snap and stepped forward to punt, but he caught Brown by surprise when he took off around the left side for a 5-yard gain. Racing back to the backfield for another punting try, he barely arrived as the ball was snapped. Carl grabbed the ball in mid-air and headed right for another 10 yards.

The team was already set when Carl jumped back into formation. This time, both Benton Bangs and he slammed straight into the line, only to have Durham slide into the middle on a delay for another 3 yards.

From there, the team went to work. Each time, the runs worked toward the spot with the greatest weakness. Defenders, who were used to fighting against a directional block, were left confused, given that there was no set pattern—only repeated pressure. Again and again, the runs came—the team lining up as quickly as the last play had finished. But Coach Dietz had worked in a bit of a surprise. On a special signal, the line would not press forward, but stand firm. Instead of the run coming, Quarterback Durham would drop back for a pass.

Looking to the left, Durham saw Loomis lined up and ready. Giving the special signal, he dropped back and quickly tossed the ball toward his receiver. Durham never saw the speedy Brown freshman defender, Clair Purdy, who intercepted the ball out of the air and raced 25 yards the other way before the mud and a push from a frustrated Durham brought him down.

Onto the field came the Brown offensive for another round.

There was no surprise about who would be getting this ball. Brown quickly snapped and handed off to Fritz Pollard for his first carry of the game. Hack Applequist grabbed onto the speedy runner's legs, but he was tossed aside like a rag doll. Pollard would sprint for an easy 15-yard gain before being dragged down by half of the Washington State squad. Back in the huddle, Applequist could only shake his head.

Brown began to go to work. Every time its players tried to run outside, the extra Washington State defenders drove them back inside. Their progress had been slowed when Bull Durham on the sideline noticed something odd. The young Brown quarterback, Purdy, was extra busy trying to dry off his hands. As a quarterback, Durham knew exactly what that meant. Purdy needed dry hands to pass the ball. Racing to tell Dietz, the coach quickly sent his quarterback into the game as a defender with the news.

It was hard for the Washington State defenders not to go after Pollard, who crashed into the line. But the hand off was a fake. Instead, Brown was doing to Washington State what Washington State had tried to do to Brown. Planting his foot, Brown quarterback Clair Purdy showed why he was given the starting job as a freshman and shot the ball out like a cannon to a wide open receiver. But the joy of success quickly disappeared as the speedy Bull Durham grabbed the ball out of the air in a true moment of irony, having been picked off moments earlier by Purdy himself.

Brown had driven the ball deep into Washington State territory, Clearly, this game was going to be a closely matched contest.

Washington State came back with a fury. To the fans, it seemed like a mad rush into the middle. As quickly as they attacked the line, players were back up and over the ball, ready to strike again. Down the field they moved—Carl Dietz smashing through the line for 10 yards—Benton Bangs for just a few—then Hanley tried his hand.

But it was the big fullback Carl Dietz who had the advantage.

Washington State knew it could now run the football.

From the sideline, Coach Dietz saw the defensive backs for Brown cheating up to the line of scrimmage. Grabbing Loomis, he sent him in with orders to launch another pass. This time, he was convinced it would work. On the snap, Durham grabbed the ball and deftly faked the handoff inside to the charging Carl Dietz. Loomis sprinted down the right side. Durham smiled as he launched the ball deep down the field for what appeared to be an easy touchdown. Looking back, Loomis reached out his arms to cradle the ball some 30 yards down the field.

Suddenly, a flash appeared in front of Loomis and the ball seemingly disappeared.

In the world of college football, athleticism can sometimes overcome the best schemes and surprise plays. So it was this day because Brown Coach Robinson substituted Fritz Pollard into the defensive backfield for his tremendous speed and athletic ability.

Brown had intercepted the ball on its own 25-yard line.

On the Washington sidelines, the team could not believe what had happened. Running off the field, Durham came up to Coach Dietz, looking for guidance. In a calm demeanor, the coach softly shook his head and smiled.

An excited Fritz Pollard was eager to get back into the action. He had just stopped Washington State's sustained drive and wanted to move the ball down the field himself. But just as quick as the hole in the line opened up, it seemed there were players falling over and clutching onto his clothes. The muddy field prevented him from using his strength to push past their weak grabs. On tackles, Washington State seemed to send everybody into the action to make sure Pollard wasn't going anywhere, even to the point of piling everyone on him.

In the Brown huddle, Pollard complained, "If it rains any harder, I might actually drown under those guys." As a testament to the truth of his words, Pollard's face and helmet were soaking wet with mud. On paper, Brown would seem to have the advantage in moving the ball. But on the field, Brown looked to be in slow motion compared to the rapid play calling of Washington State.

By the end of the half, Brown put together a decent run. A combination of runs and the occasional pass were enough to keep the drive moving. Pollard was being held in check, but not without a cost to the players. Despite Coach Dietz's continuous substitutions, several of his key players began to tire. On fourth down, with 8 yards to go inside the Washington State 40-yard line, Brown decided to go for it. Dropping back to pass, Clair Purdy tossed the ball out to the speedy halfback, Andrews, but it was overthrown.

Washington State's players began to rush off the field when a yellow flag on the ground caused them to stop in their tracks. Zimmerman had grabbed the receiver as he went outside.

"Defensive Holding," announced the referee. That would back the ball up 15 yards. More importantly, Brown would keep the ball now, at the Washington State 20-yard line.

Fritz Pollard seemed to be as fresh as when the game started. Repeatedly, he slammed into the line, but he could not gain any traction on the wet turf. Yet, through his sheer athleticism, he was able to pick up 3 yards here, another 4 there, and Brown was threatening to score with the ball on the Washington State 6-yard line.

Back in the huddle, Washington State tried to brace itself for the expected blast from Pollard. That's when the freshman linebacker noticed the same thing Durham had seen earlier. Brown Quarterback Purdy was wiping off his hands.

"They're going to pass," said Fishback.

With that, the team decided to gamble and go with a play it had used against Oregon called the linebacker blast. Defenders would push the offensive linemen to the side, leaving a hole for the linebacker to shoot through. If it worked, they would drop the quarterback for a loss. If it were a running play, Fishback would be one-on-one against a charging Pollard.

For a brief moment, Ronald Fishback feared he had made a dreadful mistake. On the snap, Brown's quarterback, Purdy, put the ball into the arms of Pollard, who smiled as the giant hole opened up on the right side of the line. Committed to the play, Fishback sprinted straight into the hole, bracing for a tremendous collision. Time seemed to slow down from all the adrenaline coursing through his body. Suddenly, the ball was pulled away as Pollard lowered his head to set a block onto the speedy Fishback. But the youngster had speed of his own; he side-stepped past Pollard like a deflected missile.

Quarterback Purdy never had a chance. Fishback would drop him from behind for a loss. Washington State would take over on downs. Brown's best chance in the game so far had been squandered as the half came to an end.

On the sidelines, the entire team leaped with excitement. Even Coach Dietz himself got caught up in the emotion and raced out to greet each of the defenders personally and shake their hands.

Both teams would race into the locker rooms, tied at zero to zero.

Pullman

The emotions among the fans in Pasadena were echoed one thousand miles away in Pullman as the dispatches could not come fast enough. Not a word could be heard as the football on the wall was parked inside the Washington State 10-yard line. Who would have believed that such simple words could carry so much weight?

"Quarterback sacked on fourth down. Brown stopped. Washington State takes over."

Fans jumped up and down, matching the emotions felt by those a thousand miles away. As halftime struck, you could see the relief in the fans' postures. Many slumped back in their chairs, emotionally spent. The game was only halfway finished.

For once, Cora Nessly got to relax. The electric teletype machine kicked out each message far faster than she ever could have kept up with a keypad. But it was still her job to verify each message before it was raced out the door to be read immediately. Every time she looked outside, it seemed the crowd kept growing larger. The sounds of cheering fans echoing through the hills of the Palouse had become a siren call. New fans seemed to arrive every minute, still memorized by this new technology that allowed them to know the results of the game almost instantly.

Halftime

The locker room was filled with the smell of wet wool pants and sweaty men. The heavy humidity had turned the windows into a gray misty fog. Doc Bohler had a system in place where every player stripped off his jersey and replaced it with a relatively dry one. Each player had dry socks to put on as well. The smell of wet cotton and wool filled the room as the uniforms dried on clotheslines hung next to a roaring potbelly stove. Granted, the temperatures outside were not all that cold compared to Pullman, but wet clothing has a way of pulling the heat out of a person's body. The game was not long in when players had abandoned their wool blankets left soaking wet.

In his typical style, Coach Dietz wandered around the players, asking them questions and offering individualized answers. So far, his team was performing admirably. Looking at Ace Clark, he knew his captain had his hands full playing against Brown's Mark Farnum, an All-American lineman of great notoriety. Surprisingly, Fritz Pollard had not been a factor.

Like his mentor and coach Pop Warner before him, Dietz was not much for making halftime speeches, but this time things felt different. Dietz truly believed the second half would belong to them. He had seen the Brown linemen dropping to their knees with the fatigue from the relentless Washington State pace. But how could he convince his players? As halftime came to a close, and men began to don jerseys and lace up shoes, the coach knew what they needed was one last rally together.

Dietz reflected briefly on the end of this grand journey, "These next thirty minutes you will remember for the rest of your lives," he said. Players looked as if he were speaking to them one on one. "We have come so far, you and I."

With an emotion he had not shown all season, Dietz called out, "This is your time. This is your chance to stand among the greatest men who have ever played this game." His voice was now rising into a renewed sense of bravado.

"This is your Chance...for Glory!"

The men around him didn't cheer. Instead, they looked at each other with a shared smile. They too now believed this day would be theirs for the taking.

Brown

On the Brown side of the field, the confidence the team carried into the game remained. Coach Robinson's message was one of "stay the course." He believed the playmaking that had brought them here would carry the team to victory.

The coach knew his team's fate lay in the hands of his best player. His halftime message was clear—it would be Pollard's time to shine. But as the Brown team came onto the field, the respite from the weather disappeared as the heaviest rains began to fall.

It would be a long and soggy day.

Second Half

Washington State would take the opening kick-off. Carl Dietz grabbed the ball and barreled straight ahead nearly 25 yards to the 40-yard line. Bull Durham came onto the field and signaled to his backs that Carl would be taking this first snap. Durham got Carl's attention and gave a glance over to the right side of the line where Clark and Applequist had been cooking something up.

"Ready down…" said Durham. Both Clark and Applequist stood up and made a complete shift. "Set… hut, hut," said Durham. The ball snapped; he spun around and drove it into Carl's stomach. Just as he hit the line, a large hole opened up, through which the fullback scampered for an easy 5 yards.

Racing back to the line of scrimmage, Durham called out his familiar "Down—set, hut, hut." But his two linemen didn't have a chance to get set when the ball was snapped; the referee called Washington State for not having six men on the line of scrimmage.

Durham settled down, knowing the penalty was on him, his linemen likely giving him a peeved stare. Two more tries off the right side, and Carl Dietz picked up another 12 yards, but because of the penalty, they would need to punt.

Carl Dietz was frustrated. They had a combination working that could move the ball down the field, but here they were having to punt. Catching the snap, Carl smashed the punt farther than he had ever kicked before. The blast caught Fritz Pollard off guard as he turned quickly to race backwards; the kick carried an unbelievable 55 yards in the air. Carl Dietz stood on the field, not wanting to leave. Coach Dietz saw his intensity and decided to leave him in the game as linebacker.

As Brown snapped the ball, Carl Dietz took off like a shot into the line. It was as if he had seen where the play was going before it actually developed. His speedy play instantly inspired the team to step it up. Brown didn't even know what had hit it. Fritz Pollard barely made it to the line of scrimmage while it looked like Washington State had extra players leaking past their vaunted offensive line.

With a short punt by Brown, Washington State would try again, this time with the series starting inside Brown territory.

Carl Dietz was already lined up when the offense arrived over the ball. The younger freshman, Ralph Boone, had come into the game to give the team three running backs. True to Coach Dietz strategy, the running duties would be shared to keep players fresh. Boone struck twice for short yardage, but on third down with four to go, Durham had noticed that Brown was setting its tackle to the outside. Calling his own number, Durham took off like he was headed outside, then cut back into the middle of the line and was nearly off to the races, until a late shoelace tackle brought him down after an 8-yard gain.

The referee spotted the ball on the Brown 24-yard line. Washington State was on the move.

Carl Dietz took the ball up the middle, for no gain. Heading to the backfield, he stopped, realizing that Basil Doane had come in to relieve him. But Doane had something else. He brought with him a surprise play. It was a reverse where the backfield would all run to the left, then hand the ball to the speedy Ray Loomis, who would race back the other way. The play worked perfectly. Nearly the entire Brown team was shifting the wrong way when Loomis raced back in the other direction. Unfortunately, just as he turned the corner around the line, his footing slipped, costing him what should have been a sure touchdown. Still—it was good for another 5 yards, and Washington State was knocking on the door from the 14-yard line.

Heavy rains only added to the panic being felt by Brown. Washington State hardly noticed with the end zone just ahead. Benton Bangs took the ball, put his head down, then smashed inside with hopes of slipping through.

But a wet football can be an ugly device to try and hold. Benton Bangs promptly fumbled the ball. Brown would recover on its own 11-yard line.

On the sidelines, the team was agitated, frustrated, even bitter that it could come so close, only to be denied again. Coach Dietz showed an even calmer side that quickly spread to the rest of his team.

After one failed run off tackle with Fritz Pollard, Brown decided to play a field position game again, and promptly lined up to punt the ball away. Carl Dietz was eager to get back in the game, but it would be Durham who would get the call.

On the kick, Durham brought the ball back to the Brown 40-yard line, to almost the exact spot as before. Carl Dietz noticed a dry spot on the field. Grabbing onto his quarterback, Durham, he knew he could drive a key block in that very spot. Durham looked down and saw what he saw. Smiling, he whispered the idea in Hack's ear, and then to the youngster Boone. On the snap, the gap opened again between the two Washington State linemen, only this time, the linebacker who was supposed to fill the gap found himself facing Carl Dietz with a full head of steam.

What few saw was the smaller Ralph Boone shooting through the gap and running into open field. Unfortunately, the dry ground didn't last far, and Boone was tripped up by a large puddle that slowed him enough for the Brown defender to catch up. Still, the ball had been moved 21 yards. Washington State was knocking on the door again, and its players were sprinting to the line with a new sense of urgency.

On the other side of the ball, the play put a dark cloud over the Brown team. Quick to snap the ball, Durham spun around and tucked the ball into Carl's hands. Off to the left, he squeezed through the gap for an important 4-yard gain. Again and again, the Washington State offense hit the line faster than any other time that year. Three plays later, freshman Ralph Boone found himself standing alone in the end zone. Washington State had scored. Durham made sure the ball dropped square through the uprights for the extra point.

Washington State 7, Brown 0.

Pullman

What few fans remained on the outskirts of Pullman knew something amazing was going on downtown. Mayor Harley Johnson was reading the most important dispatch of the game. Already, the Western Union Telegram machine had fed over a dozen dispatches, but it would be this latest one that would long be remembered.

"Bangs over the right guard for 3," began Johnson. "Dietz over the left guard for 9. Boone around the left side for 4 and the touchdown."

The result was a simultaneous, single voice that boomed its way across the hills of the Palouse. Fans jumped up and down. People hugged—often people they'd never met. Fans celebrated as if they themselves had just scored.

Pasadena

Coach William Dietz shook the hands of every player as they came off. The momentum had clearly shifted to his side of the field. The job now was to keep things lighthearted and moving ahead. He knew that, on the other side of the field, desperation and exhaustion were working against Brown.

Coach Robinson tried to rally his team, calling in substitutes to give his players a rest. But what he gained in energy was not returned in talent. The rains and the relentless attack had taken its toll on the team. After Washington State kicked off, Brown could never quite get going. Three plays later—it would be forced to punt.

The offensive unit for Washington State was on the march again. Bangs, Boone, and Carl Dietz repeatedly pressed into the line and then jumped back up to run immediately. Yet it was Dietz who carried the team. Once again, Washington State walked the ball down to the 14-yard line, where the quarter came to an end. On the second play, Bangs fumbled again inside the 10-yard line.

Sprinting back to the sidelines, Bangs was met by Coach Dietz, who would not let his speedy back get down on himself. Smiling, Dietz even patted Bangs on the back. This was why Bangs loved playing for this man. Dietz exuded true leadership by being strong, yet humble in his approach; not one of his players would ever feel diminished or suffer the brunt of a public tirade witnessed by people on both sides of the field.

The rest of the game was caught up in a similar cycle. Brown would give up the ball after three downs. Washington State would drive to inside the 20-yard line. Not once in the second half did the play go onto the Washington State side of the field. A missed field goal try was the only bright spot in the game for Brown.

Carl Dietz ambled back to the huddle quickly, as if to say, "I'm ready to go to work." And work, he did. For most of the drive, Carl would slam his body into the line, forcing his way into the slim holes created by his offense. Ron Fishback had yet to leave the field for a single play, yet he looked just as strong as he did on the very first series. Clark and he had done a masterful job in keeping the Brown All-American tackle at bay.

The trio of backs seemed unstoppable. Washington State drove the ball down the field in small chunks. Three yards here, 4 yards there, and suddenly, it was on the goal line again. On his second try, Carl Dietz dropped his head and drove his legs as hard as he could until suddenly the forces that were pushing back seemed to vanish as he burst into the end zone. Force of habit had him running back into place for the next play, but he had to stop and pause—looking first at the football in his hand, then up at the scoreboard. He had just scored.

Only a smiling Durham, who needed the ball for the extra point, could take this moment away. With the kick, Washington State had taken a 14-0 lead with less than a minute to play, but in reality, the game was over.

As the final gun sounded, the team raced to the center of the field. None of them wanted this moment to end. Fans began to rush into the fray to be part of the celebration. On the sideline, watching it all, was the injured actor Tom Moore cheering wildly from his wheelchair. Doctors had declared that Moore was O.K., but the studio had insisted he use the device as a precaution.

Coach Dietz stood quietly on the sidelines. These men had done all that he had asked. They had performed all that he had dreamed could be possible. He closed his eyes and breathed in the air around him, wanting to remember everything about this moment for all time.

Newspapers across the country declared Washington State to be among the best, if not *the* best in the land. *The Los Angeles Examiner*, in its report of the game, said in part: "Washington, accustomed to using an open form of attack, showed her great adaptability by changing her style to meet the conditions, and rather than take any chances with fancy handling of the slippery ball." Howard Angus, sports editor of the *Los Angeles Times*, said, "Brown can thank the gods of luck that the score was not 28 to 0."

Dietz would give all the credit for the win to his players.

They had all traveled to this distant land to compete on a national stage. They had done what few ever dreamed possible. And they would forever be seen as champions.

Dance of Champions

If the Hotel Maryland seemed posh, then the Hotel Green was simply decadent. Everywhere you looked were trimmings done in dark woods, marble, and velvet. Long tapestries that spoke of wealth and luxury were hung along most of the walls. Paintings and large vases were on display that, had they been given closer examination, would have revealed themselves to be the work of true masters.

A rousing round of cheers and applause erupted as the team entered the ballroom. It was the official Tournament of Roses Ball, where the men on the field were treated as celebrities in the eyes of those who often used celebrity status to gauge a person's worth. Instantly, as the Washington State men entered the room, it seemed as if a dancing partner were all but pre-ordained. A number of women, sporting the latest fashions, all emerged before these northern gentlemen in hopes of fostering their attentions.

A grumbling bookie arrived at the dance, ready to pay off the players' winnings. By game time, Washington State was nearly a three-to-one underdog. A number of the players would be headed home with a considerable amount of money in their pockets. It would be an evening filled with grand toasts, along with some wild entertainment by a young woman dancer and, of course, a late evening of music and dancing for the "National Champions from Washington State College."

Champions Return

By the time the reports of the game filled the newspaper, the team was nearly home. As they had during the winter break, Lillian McDonald and Helen Quarrels gathered together to read the latest news of their boys in California. Back now in Pullman, the morning was spent getting ready for their arrival. All preparations for the new semester would be put on hold until the team arrived from California.

"The Tournament of Roses Ball followed the banquet and the football men were heroes in the eyes of the vast throng," the pair read. Both had to be somewhat astonished at the next passage, "The players sitting in a huge square within which Miss Gail Langdon performed her famous Oriental dance of the Soul's Journey. Speaking of the dancer the Hotel Green Daily remarks: Miss Langdon's costume was-well, conspicuous by its absence, but her smile makes up for everything."

The two had to share a smile, wondering just how these two conservative gentlemen would react in the retelling of this tale. But whatever humor was found would likely give way to a fear of the unknown. Both would soon learn just how much the trip had changed these two men and the love they shared.

Accolades from across the nation began pouring in. Telegrams arrived almost immediately from political and industry leaders. The Mayor of Spokane wrote, "All Spokane congratulates the best football team in the United States. You have put the Northwest on the map to stay." While the president of Western Insurance wrote "…congratulations on your victory, the West is the best. Show Dietz where to sign."

Whatever dreams President Enoch Bryan may have had to bring prominence and recognition to his Washington State College had worked well beyond his imagination.

Trains

Before the team would turn back toward Pullman, the royal treatment of the Tournament of Roses committee would continue. First stop, a lavish party in Tijuana, Mexico, taking in a special day of horse racing and the county fair, with the players hailed as champions. But their celebrations would continue all the way back up the coast. Washington State's victory did more than just capture national honors; it was seen as bringing true legitimacy to football on the West Coast. In San Francisco, the exclusive Olympic Club opened its doors for a large event, while in Portland, the players were the guests of the Hotel Oregon and the Multnomah Club.

In Los Angeles, Coach Dietz had said his goodbyes at the train station. "I wish I could stay longer, but I have a telegram to write," he said as he turned to walk away from the station. He wrote the note, knowing full well Doc Bohler wouldn't be home for a few days. "Accept terms..." wrote Dietz. Before he left, Enoch Bryan had tendered Dietz an offer to return as the head coach for Washington State for the unbelievable sum of $4,000. It would make him the highest paid coach in the West. Football, it seems, was an up-and-coming sport, with colleges negotiating to create a new Pacific Coast Conference to include teams from Washington, Oregon, and California.

As the train moved past Portland, one last piece of business was left to conclude the season—the election of a captain for the coming year.

The vote wasn't even close. The players unanimously elected Benton Bangs as captain for the 1916 season. There was even talk that the University of Washington had relented and would play in Pullman after all.

Pullman

Making the last mile toward the Pullman station, players were visibly confused by a peculiar sound that emerged. Imperceptible at first, it grew clearly louder as the cars slowed. As the train rolled into the station, it was clear what was creating this tremendous wall of sound—cheering fans. As far as the eyes could see, the station was packed with wildly excited fans, all craning their necks for a look at these returning champions. There wasn't a rooftop or sidewalk that wasn't packed with wall-to-wall fans.

Carl Dietz was the first to step out, blinking wildly as thousands of waiting fans roared even louder. As the MVP of the Tournament of Roses game, the team had given him the honor of being the first off the train. The players could barely make their way through the station; then suddenly, a long row of young men from the college, each pulling on the same rope, could be seen dragging a toboggan. Soon, four other sleds appeared to carry the team all the way up the snow-covered hills to Washington State College.

Along the way, hundreds of fans stood waiting patiently in the snow for the chance to cheer home their team. Large banners were painted calling the team "Our Champions," and "Champions of the World." Once on campus, each player was carried to Bryan Hall and greeted by the man who had started it all, Enoch Bryan. Newspapers of the day would call this "the wildest and most enthusiastic, demonstration of unqualified joy in the annals of Pullman's history."

Of the experience, Asa Clark would say, "the best feature of it all is getting home."

But there was one other memory Asa Clark would long remember. Lillian McDonald had waited patiently for several hours, all for this one moment. She needed to look into Ace Clark's eyes for herself to see the truth. She believed that in that instant, the course of her life might be set. His eyes would answer for her the all important question: Was he still the man she sent off a few weeks ago, or had the experience made him into something different?

As Asa Clark stepped out of the train, his eyes scanned the area, searching. Spotting Lillian, it was as if all the excitement around him had disappeared. Moving directly into her arms, his kiss told her all she needed to know. Smiling together, arm in arm, the pair jumped on one of the toboggans as thousands of fans followed behind, cheering their returning champions up the hill and back to school.

The players were back to their college homes, with the new semester upon them. Campus life would soon return to its normal pace.

But for the players and fans alike, their lives would be forever changed.

CHAPTER 9
ENDINGS

DUPLICITY ENDS

Olympia, Washington
February, 2, 1917

Governor Ernest Lister's patience had come to an end.

There seemed to be no stopping this feud between the University of Washington and Washington State College. Nothing had worked. As the legislative session drew to a close, he brought both presidents to Olympia and locked them into a room with Washington State lawmakers in hopes a compromise could be hammered out. Yet after two all-night sessions, both sides remained hardened in their position, with charges of bad faith now being levied on both sides. Like a father stepping in between two arguing children, Lister knew it was up to him to settle this fight.

Gathered into his office at 4:00 a.m., the governor looked across the desk at the two solemn men. UW President Henry Suzzallo and WSC President Ernest Holland, who once had called themselves friends, were so embittered that neither would even look at the other. Each had waged a vigorous campaign: The U of W had fought for exclusivity; WSC had fought for respectability. It was a frustrating session for lawmakers who believed the issue had been settled at the end of the 1916 legislative session. Washington State's supporters had rolled into that New Year filled with the excitement of its Rose Bowl victory and national prominence on the athletic field. Waiting for the end of the session, the Duplicity Committee gave lawmakers its final report.

But that turned out to be only the beginning.

Over the last year, both men had engaged in a continuous lobbying effort. The debate had wearied lawmakers, especially with the country on the verge of war. America had just cut off diplomatic ties with Germany, a final act that would lead to the country's full military involvement.

Lister didn't need to say much.

That he had insisted both men come alone to his office at the end of a long night said more than words would ever say. Looking at each president individually, he simply asked, "Will you accept my decision?"

Neither was offered the chance to object.

Each simply answered, "Yes."

With that, the governor handed each a simple sheet containing his compromise, saying, "Major line to the university—service line at the state college." As the two men read the final document, it became clear that Washington State College would keep its federal endowments and extension funding, while retaining its right to teach many of the core classes currently offered. The University of Washington would have exclusive rights to law, journalism, and aeronautic engineering. WSC was given veterinary medicine and almost anything related to agriculture. Both schools would be allowed to teach liberal arts, pure sciences, and architecture. To help keep the peace, a Joint-Board of Higher Curricula would be established with leadership from both schools meeting to make recommendations to the legislature.

A newspaper reporter, J.W. Gilbert, wrote, "Collectively, the assembly heaved a sigh of relief when it was over." Rules were suspended, allowing the bills to be swept through both the House and Senate and over to the governor for his immediate signature. The legislative fight was now over. On the football field, the competition between the two would now resume.

UW Coach Gil Dobie would be coaxed into returning for one more season, sweeping through the newly formed Pacific Coast Conference with a 6-0-1 record. Washington fans returned to the game, even launching an official fight song, "Bow Down to Washington," written by a student as part of a contest, with a few lines of the song honoring Dobie. True to his word, Dobie would not see UW play WSC until the year after he left.

Washington State would not join the Pacific Coast Conference until the following year. It wasn't until 1918 that the rivalry game, The Apple Cup, would resume. Under Dietz, Washington State would win the game 14-0.

During his three years, Dietz compiled a record of 17-2-1. There was talk he would remain the coach forever. But the specter of war soon haunted his career. With the outbreak of World War I, Washington State College joined other universities in cancelling the 1918 season. Many of the WSC players had enlisted together in the Marines, so when Dietz learned they were playing for the Corp, he made his way to Mare Island to become their coach.

Dietz would spend the rest of his career coaching football at a variety of schools, including Purdue, Louisiana Tech, Wyoming, and Albright College, even taking over as the head coach of the Boston Braves football team in 1933 and '34. According to family members, George Marshall Preston, the team owner, changed the Boston team's name to the Redskins based on Dietz's leadership. Even though William Dietz coached the team for just two seasons, the name would stick. In 1935, Preston moved the team to Washington D.C., where it remains as the Washington Redskins to this day. Dietz also made a living as an artist. He produced twenty-seven drawings to serve as illustrations in the definitive football coaching book, *Football for Coaches and Players,* by his former mentor, Pop Warner.

The Carlisle connection would continue to serve Washington State College. Two more players from the Carlisle team who played West Point would follow Dietz to WSC. Gus Welch, the Carlisle quarterback, would come to Washington State College to coach for four seasons from 1919 until 1922 with a respectable 16-10-1 record. Next was Albert Exendine, who would coach WSC from 1923 until 1925; he was so renowned for his wide open offenses that he was once scolded by his former coach, Pop Warner: "Ex, you will become a great football coach if you can remember that football is football, and basketball is basketball."

But the record of either coach doesn't compare to the one amassed by William Dietz.

The teams of that 1916 Rose Bowl were celebrated long after the game. The Tournament of Roses Committee paid to have remaining members and their spouses back to celebrate the 40th Anniversary of the Tournament of Roses East-West Game, and *Sports Illustrated* lined both sides up for a large centerfold photo.

Walter Eckersall, a three-time All-American from Chicago who served as the referee for the Rose Bowl game, said, "In my opinion, the Washington State College team…is as strong an aggregation as I have ever seen this year." Powerful words from a well-respected football figure of the day who had refereed for Cornell and other East Coast powerhouses. He added, "The Washington State eleven must be ranked as one of the best elevens in the country."

Most importantly, the reputation of West Coast football was now established, having been tarnished by Stanford's humiliating Rose Bowl defeat back in 1902.

As for the Tournament of Roses committee, the game was a disaster. By some estimates, the losses were well over $11,000, just under what they had paid to the two teams to travel. The naysayers believed they had been proven right. But before they could vote to cancel the game permanently, one of the committee members, J.J. Mitchel, a popular Canadian Hockey player, announced to the media that the game was a success and that plans were underway for the next game January 1, 1917—a bold move that many believe saved the game. When both of Pasadena's two newspapers came out with strong editorial support for the contest, the committee felt it had no choice but to continue with this new tradition of football. The next season, despite the rains, some 25,000 fans filled the stands, not wanting to miss out like many had the year before.

The legacy of the Tournament of Roses game had begun. Decades later, Washington State graduate and ABC sportscaster Keith Jackson would coin the phrase, "The Granddaddy of Them All," a title that remains to this day.

Love and Marriage

In the weeks following their return from the Rose Bowl, two players made good on their pledges of love. On a concrete bench outside the administration building, Asa Clark would make his and Lillian McDonald's engagement official. In a college tradition of the day, Asa presented Lillian with his Kappa Sigma pin. Given upon initiation, the pin stood as a symbol of reverence, with the intent it be surrendered back to the fraternity on the member's death. Since the pin was considered the property of the house, the significance was equivalent to that of a promise ring or engagement.

Asa Clark

Asa Clark and Lillian McDonald would be wed shortly after graduation, settling on the Clark homestead farm north of Pullman. Clark would go on to become one of the most prominent farmers in Whitman County, and he served with distinction as Washington State Senator for fifteen years, even serving as an agricultural ambassador to the former Soviet USSR. Clark Hall on the WSU campus is named in his honor.

Benton Bangs

Benton Bangs would give his fraternity pin to Helen Quarrels the day he returned from the Rose Bowl game. Bangs' playing days continued well after college. He would play on the Mare Island team for Coach Dietz, after enlisting in the Marine Corps. After the war, he would follow his grandfather into the apple business, becoming one of the largest fruit tract owners in Chelan, Washington. With a hand for politics, he would be elected as a Chelan County Commissioner.

Enoch Bryan

After President Enoch Bryan retired, he went on to make an unsuccessful run for the U.S. Senate. Many historians credit him for being the man who built Washington State College to a respectable level, in the sciences, in infrastructure, and in reputation. He would spend many of his last days back at Washington State where he would pen his memoirs, stating that he believed "duplicity" had been the greatest threat ever faced by his beloved college.

The clock tower and the hall in the middle of the Washington State University campus bear his name.

John Frederick "Doc" Bohler

Doc Bohler served Washington State College with distinction, staying on as the athletic director well into his sixties. He also served as the head basketball coach from 1908 to 1926, with a record of 226-177. Following the success of football, his basketball team would go on to win the National Championship the following year. He also served for four years as the baseball coach.

Among Bohler's greatest achievements would be the establishment of the first intramural sports programs, which encouraged all

Washington State students to become physically engaged in athletics as part of their educational experience.

Bohler Gymnasium on the WSU campus is named in his honor.

Arthur "Bull" Durham

Quarterback Bull Durham was among the first to enlist in the Navy when the U.S. entered the war. A career military man, he served with distinction in two wars. Along the way, he would be awarded the Bronze star and the Legion of Merit and be made an honorary commander of a military division of the British Empire.

Durham would retire from the Navy at the rank of commodore.

Clarence "Zim" Zimmerman

Clarence Zimmerman was named one of Washington State College's first ever All-Americans for football. After enlisting in the armed services, he would later return to Washington State College to finish his degree in 1924.

He served as a teacher, a sports administrator, and a high school principal in Yakima, Washington.

Dick "Milk" Hanley

Dick Hanley would play for Dietz at Mare Island, and he stayed in the Marine Corps long enough to become the coach of the team. His affinity for the game would last a lifetime. His illustrious career in the game would include serving as the head football coach of the El Toro Marines, the Haskell Indians, and for Northwestern University.

LeRoy "Roy" Hanley

Leroy Hanley also played for the Mare Island team. Like his brother, he too remained a student of the game. Hanley would stay in the Marines long enough to retire as a colonel. He would go on to become the head football coach for Boston University.

Alfred Langdon

Langdon would enlist in the armed forces the summer after the Rose Bowl game. The Army allowed him to return in the fall to complete his studies. Langdon even played for Washington State in the 1916 season.

Following the war, Langdon would go on an extended visit to South America, telling his family it was a promise he had made to himself to see the places he had read about as a child.

Harry "Hack" Applequist

Harry A. Applequist would receive All-America honors, and he was later named to the all-time Rose Bowl team by Los Angeles columnist Bill Henry. After World War I, Applequist returned to WSU as an assistant football coach, serving from 1920 through 1925. He also served as baseball coach from 1923-26, with a record of 66-29-1, only to be succeeded as coach by "Buck" Bailey.

Applequist would move to Sacramento, where he became a well-respected educator. Among his duties, he rebuilt a floundering Sacramento High football program, and then he served as the head football and basketball coach at Sacramento City College from 1929-41. He would remain as an administrator with the Sacramento School District until his retirement in 1956. The author of three books, he was elected to the Sacramento Hall of Fame and received an Emeritus Award from the U.S. Department of Health, Physical Education, and Recreation.

Carl Dietz

At the outbreak of World War I, Carl Dietz was quick to enlist. He died in 1924 from an illness he contracted during the war.

Ronald Fishback

Ronald Fishback was the son of Washington State Insurance Commissioner H.O. Fishback, and the younger brother of WSC football star Tom Fishback. He would have graduated in 1919 had he not enlisted in the army in 1917 to join the war effort. Following the war, Fishback would settle in the Cowlitz County area where he would pass away in 1929.

Fritz Pollard

Fritz Pollard would be the first African-American ever named to the Walter Camp All American team. He would go on to become the first African-American to play professional football for the Akron Pros, leading the team to the NFL (APFA) championship in 1920. The following year, he would both play and serve as co-coach for the team, officially becoming the game's first black football coach.

Pollard was inducted into the NFL Hall of Fame in 2005.

His son Fritz Pollard, Jr., would become a champion in track and field, winning a bronze medal in 110 meter hurdles at the 1936 Summer Olympics in Berlin, despite tripping over the final hurdle.

William Kruegel

William Kruegel, the finance officer from WSC who went with the team to Pasadena, would serve the university with distinction for several decades.

Kruegel Hall is named in his honor.

Wallace Wade

Wallace Wade, who played on the line for Brown, would return to the Rose Bowl a decade later as the head coach of the Alabama Crimson Tide. His Alabama teams of 1925, 1926, and 1930, were recognized as national champions. In all, Wade would coach five Rose Bowls for Alabama and Duke, including the 1942 game, which was relocated from Pasadena to Durham, North Carolina, after the attack on Pearl Harbor. Duke's football stadium was renamed in his honor as Wallace Wade Stadium in 1967.

Pug Barnes

The most infamous of the early college "Rooter Kings," Pug Barnes will be remembered for his never-ending energy and his bawdy football songs. Sadly, Barnes would come down with pneumonia shortly after the Rose Bowl game and would pass away a few weeks later in January of 1916.

Epilogue

William "Lone Star" Dietz would return to Washington State College for a visit in 1956. It was there he would accept the gift the school had long wanted to present—a wool blanket. A mark of distinction he had bestowed on his players.

At the age of eighty, William Dietz would pass away nearly penniless in a small Pennsylvania town. His former Albright College friends purchased for him a burial plot in the Schwartzwald Cemetery. Among his final wishes were that his ashes be spread at The Rose Bowl, but that request was never granted.

A simple marker sits atop his gravesite. It reads:

WILLIAM DIETZ
"Lone Star"
August 16, 1885
July 20, 1964
"COACH"

BIBLIOGRAPHY

Chapter 1: Beginnings

The Game

Historical notes from http://www.historyorb.com/events/date/1912

"I so loved the bodily contact...": Gene Schoor, *100 Years of Army Navy Football*, (New York: Holt and Company, 1989) p. 47-48; also: Sally Jenkins, *The Real All Americans*, (New York, Broadway Books, 2007) p. 282

Five thousand fans, *New York Times*, November 10, 1912

Two Yale Players were hospitalized... Sally Jenkins, *The Real All Americans*, (New York, Broadway Books, 2007) p. 281

Death of players: *The Shame of College Sports*, October, 2011

"I so loved the bodily contact...": Gene Schoor, *100 Years of Army Navy Football*, (New York: Holt and Company, 1989) p. 47-48; also: Sally Jenkins, *The Real All Americans*, (New York, Broadway Books, 2007) p. 282

The players had long since.... Sally Jenkins, *The Real All Americans*, (New York, Broadway Books, 2007) p. 1

"What's the use of crying over a few inches..." Handwritten autobiographical notes by Gus Welch, Gus Welch Papers, Special Collections, McFarlin Library, University of Tulsa. Also obituary of Welch in the *Bedford Bulletin Democrat*, February 1970

Storm clouds rolled over; *New York Times*, November 10, 1912

"Eisenhower himself had long awaited...": Kenneth S. Davis, *Dwight D. Eisenhower, Soldier, General of the Army, President-Elect, 1890-1952* (New York: Simon & Schuster, 1983), p. 49

"laced up ankle-high leather cleats with thick soles, others heavy football pants bagged": Sally Jenkins, *The Real All Americans,* (New York, Broadway Books, 2007) p. 1

Nervously paced through the locker room: Robert. W Wheeler, *Jim Thorpe: World's Greatest Athlete,* (Norman: University of Oklahoma Press, 1979) p. 128

"Your fathers and your grandfathers are the ones who fought their fathers. These men playing against you today are soldiers. They are the Long Knives. You are Indians. Tonight we will know if you are warriors": Alexander M. Weyland, *The Saga of American Football,* (New York: Macmillian company, 1955) p. 101

"I shouldn't have to prepare you for this game. Just go to your rooms and read your history books," *The Dickinsonian*, March 23, 1956 – found in the Gus Welch Papers, Special Collections, McFarlin Library, University of Tulsa

His team had been working: Pop Warner, *Football's Greatest Teacher: The Epic Biography of College Football's Winningest Coach*, edited by Mike Bynum (Langhornc, PΛ, Pop Warner Little Scholars, 1993), p. 141

Warner's most innovative scheme yet: Weyland, *The Saga of American Football*, p. 101

...from his linebacker position: Kenneth S. Davis, *Dwight D. Eisenhower, Soldier, General of the Army, President-Elect, 1890-*

1952 (New York: Simon & Schuster, 1983), p. 49

Arcasa cut up the field, Bill Crawford, *All American: The Rise and Fall of Jim Thorpe*, p. 191-192

He rumbled for 13 yards; Play-by-play sheet of Army's 1912 football season from the original files of the United States Military Academy, West Point, N.Y.

Hell's bells, Mr. Referee…: Sally Jenkins, *The Real All Americans,* (New York, Broadway Books, 2007) p. 284

Thorpe approached the referee,: Newcombe, The Best of the Athletic Boys, p. 201-202

Game details from the *New York Tribune, New York Herald*, and the *New York Times*, November 10, 1912, and Alexander Weyland, *The Saga of American Football*, (New York: Macmillan company, 1955) p. 183-86 – and Sally Jenkins, *The Real All Americans,* (New York, Broadway Books, 2007) p. 283-286

To pull this off: *Eisenhower*: Kenneth S. Davis, *Dwight D. Eisenhower: Soldier of Democracy*, (New York: Smithmark, 1995) p. 137

Eisenhower and Hobbs closed in: Davis, *Dwight D. Eisenhower*, p. 137

Stopped the instant before: Carlo D'Este, *Eisenhower: A Soldier's Life*, (New York: Holt and Company, 2003) p. 68

Plan to go after Thorpe: Joseph Cress, *The Sentinel*, "Carlisle vs. Army: 100 years later, South Central PA, November 8, 2012 http://cumberlink.com/news/local/carlisle-vs-army-years-later-game-remembered-for-celebrity-players/article_76d688fc-2a06-11e2-

a994-001a4bcf887a.html

Stopped short let them collide: Cress (see above)

Carlisle vs. Army: 100 years later, game remembered for celebrity players November 08, 2012 9:00 pm, Joseph Cress, *The Sentinel*

Shooting pain ripping… : Kenneth S. Davis, *Eisenhower: American Hero*, (New York: American Heritage, 1969) p. 23

Walter Camp, the former Yale quarterback: Jack Newcombe, *The Best of the Athletic Boys*, (Garden City, N.Y.: Doubleday, 1975) p. 202

As for Dwight..: Kenneth S. Davis, *Eisenhower: American Hero*, (New York: American Heritage, 1969) p. 23

Walter Camp listened attentively: Robert W. Wheeler, *Jim Thorpe: World's Greatest Athlete*, (Norman: University of Oklahoma Press, 1979) p. 132

Also as reference

Tom Benjey, *The Torch*, magazine of the U. S. Army War College, commemorating the 100th Anniversary of the 1912 Carlisle-Army football game

Duplicity

Grown weary: Joe Ashlock letter to Pres. Clement French, January 1956, Manuscripts, Archives, & Special Collections, Washington State University Libraries

Now at risk: Enoch Bryan, *Historical Sketch of the State College of Washington 1890-1925*, (Spokane, WA Inland American Printing, 1925) p. 382

Investigation: Bryan p. 383

That all men and women: Morrill Act July 2, 1862 National Archives

Cow College, hayseed students: Bryan, p. 382

Henry Suzzallo had been appointed: Bryan, p. 384

Letter to the state's editors: Bryan letter to Scott Bone, Editor in Chief, *Seattle Post-Intelligencer*, March 27, 1915, Manuscripts, Archives, & Special Collections, Washington State University Libraries

Bryan often contemplated: Joe Ashlock letter to Pres. Clement French, January 1956, Manuscripts, Archives, & Special Collections, Washington State University Libraries

Was there someone: Telegram to Pop Warner, March 1915, Manuscripts, Archives, & Special Collections, Washington State University Libraries

Glenn "Pop" Warner

One fateful day: Michael D. Koehler, "Jim Thorpe: Legend and Legacy," *Journal of American Indian Education*, Volume 15 Number 3 (May 1976)

Telegram to Pop Warner, March 1915, Manuscripts, Archives, & Special Collections, Washington State University Libraries

Stun the sporting world: *The Worchester Telegram*, January 22, 1913

Knew he had options: "History of Glenn Warner," *The Gazette Times*, (Pittsburgh, PA December 6, 1914) p. 20

Search

Negotiations within one month: Joe Ashlock letter to President C. Clement French, January 14, 1956 – Manuscripts, Archives, & Special Collections, Washington State University Libraries

Plenty of internal strife: Bryan, p. 392

Dietz and nine others: Letters of application and recommendation, Office of President Bryan letters, ER Wingard, February 9, 1915. Senator Sutton, February 16, 1915, Guy Lowman, February 20, 1915, Coach Wingard of Maine, March 5, 1915. Manuscripts, Archives, & Special Collections, Washington State University Libraries

Search: Joe Ashlock letter to Pres. Clement French, January 1956 , Manuscripts, Archives, & Special Collections, Washington State University Libraries

University of Washington Football

Gloomy Gil: Lynn Borland, "Legendary coach Gil Dobie's only loss at Washington: his legacy," *The Seattle Times* (Seattle WA, November 20, 2010)

Decisions

Salary of $2,250: Tom Benjey, *Keep A Goin', The Life of Lone Star Dietz*, (Carlisle, PA Tuxedo Press, 2006) p. 99

What Bryan didn't tell anyone: Bryan, p. 392

How do you feel…: Joe Ashlock letter to Pres. Clement French, January 1956 , Manuscripts, Archives, & Special Collections, Washington State University Libraries

Arrival

A lone figure: Interview with Girard Clark, son of football Captain Asa Clark, by author Pullman WA, October 18, 1997

Dietz arrived: Richard B. Fry, *The Crimson and the Gray*, 100 years with the WSU Cougars, (Pullman, WA, Washington State University Press, 1989) p. 68

Out of the void: Tom Benjey, *Keep A Goin', The Life of Lone Star Dietz*,(Carlisle, PA Tuxedo Press, 2006) p. 104

Rally

Wrapped up a package: *Pullman Herald,* August 13, 1915 front page

Eager to train: *Pullman Herald,* August 27, 1915 front page

Also noted: John Frederick Bohler Papers 1907-1956, Manuscripts, Archives, and Special Collections, Washington State University Libraries

Impressions

Well dressed: *John C. Ewers, Montana the Magazine of Western History*, Volume XXVII, Number One, Winter 1977, p. 8

Critical to success: *Pullman Herald*, September 3, 1915 p. 5

"Impressions were not good": Girard Clark, Interview with Girard Clark, son of football Captain Asa Clark, by author Pullman WA October 18, 1997

Camp

Clark's Search led him to Liberty Lake park: Al Knutsen, *The*

Splash, (Liberty Lake, WA - For the Liberty Lake Historical Society, October 30, 2014) p. 1

"More enthusiasm has been shown...": *Spokesman Chronicle*, Spokane WA September 23, 1915 p. 9

"Bohler confirms will train at Liberty Lake": *Spokesman Chronicle*, Spokane WA August 3, 1915

Richard B. Fry, *The Crimson and the Gray, 100 years with the WSU Cougars,* (Pullman, WA, Washington State University Press, 1989) p. 68

Revelry

Zimmerman and others: Girard Clark, Interview with Girard Clark, son of football Captain Asa Clark, by author Pullman WA October 18, 1997

Player descriptions: *Chinook 1917*, p. 111-119

Good condition: Asa Clark Interview with L.H. Gregory 1943 *Oregonian*, (as noted by Fry, p. 72)

Dietz drove the charges hard: John C. Ewers, *Montana the Magazine of Western History*, Volume XXVII, Number One, Winter 1977, p. 9

Chess: Girard Clark, Interview with Girard Clark, son of football Captain Asa Clark, by author Pullman WA October 18, 1997

When are we going to play football?: Asa Clark Interview with L.H. Gregory 1943 *Oregonian*, (as noted by Fry, p. 72)

Keyhole: *Chinook 1917*, p. 391

(Dietz) Story of his childhood – Richard B. Fry, *The Crimson and the Gray, 100 years with the WSU Cougars,* (Pullman, WA, Washington State University Press, 1989) p. 68

Dietz father's captivity: *Reader's Digest*, January 23, 1912, p. 160-161 (reprinted from *The New York Sun*

Stomp: Girard Clark, Interview with Girard Clark, son of football Captain Asa Clark, by author Pullman WA October 18, 1997

Day Two

Shoulder roll: Girard Clark, Interview with Girard Clark, son of football Captain Asa Clark, by author Pullman WA October 18, 1997

Offense and Defense: Girard Clark, Interview with Girard Clark, son of football Captain Asa Clark, by author Pullman WA October 18, 1997

Use the Carlisle system: *Pullman Herald*, September 3 1915 p. 5

Clark, I need you: Girard Clark, Interview with Girard Clark, son of football Captain Asa Clark, by author Pullman WA October 18, 1997

Last Days

Zimmerman a practical joker: Girard Clark, Interview with Girard Clark, son of football Captain Asa Clark, by author Pullman WA October 18, 1997

"...as good a material," *Evergreen*, September 23, 1915

Duplicity Speaks

Suzzalo speech – *Spokane Daily Chronicle*, September 9, 1915 p. 2

Return to Pullman

An energized group: *Evergreen,* September 30, 1915 front page

Chessboard: Girard Clark, Interview with Girard Clark, son of football Captain Asa Clark, by author Pullman WA October 18, 1997

Langdon center: *Pullman Herald,* September 24, 1915 front page

Alumni will play game: *Evergreen,* September 30, 1915 p. 3

Plays name for players: Girard Clark, Interview with Girard Clark, son of football Captain Asa Clark, by author Pullman WA October 18, 1997

Defense

Defense: Girard Clark, Interview with Girard Clark, son of football Captain Asa Clark, by author Pullman WA October 18, 1997

Pullman

Beginning: *Pullman Herald,* September 24, 1915 front page

Frustrated: Girard Clark, Interview with Girard Clark, son of football Captain Asa Clark, by author Pullman WA October 18, 1997

Enlisting Help

As the players: Girard Clark, Interview with Girard Clark, son of football Captain Asa Clark, by author Pullman WA October 18, 1997

Newspaper Clip

Pullman Herald, September 24, 1915 front page

Freshman-Sophomore Competition

The freshman-sophomore competition: *Evergreen*, September 30, 1915

Freshman-Sophomore Game

Evergreen, September 30, 1915 front page/last page

Fishback: Interview with Girard Clark, son of football Captain Asa Clark, by author Pullman WA October 18, 1997 and *Pullman Herald*, September 24, 1915 front page

Duplicity Continues

Spokane Daily Chronicle, August 17, 1915 p. 7

Belittling the college: Karl P Allen, Editor *Pullman Herald*, September 24, 1915 p. 17

Plenty of Spokane students attend WSU: *Pullman Herald* September 10, 1915, front page

Series of letters and telegrams from Bryan: WSU libraries, 1915 correspondence logbook for Bryan, Manuscripts and Special Collections

Alumni Game

Alumni will play: *Evergreen*, September 30, 1915 p. 3

Alumni game recap: *Evergreen*, October 7, 1915 p. 2 and *Pullman Herald*, October 8 1915 front page

Team Meeting

One comment, Practice the next day: Girard Clark, Interview with

Girard Clark, son of football Captain Asa Clark, by author Pullman WA October 18, 1997

A New Dawn

As the sun began to rise: Girard Clark, Interview with Girard Clark, son of football Captain Asa Clark, by author Pullman WA October 18, 1997

A Time Long Past

Dietz history: Rob Jackson, "Wicarhpi Isnala," *The Coffin Corner*: Vol. 26, No. 1 (2004) http://profootballresearchers.com/archives/ Website_Files/Coffin_Corner/26-01-1014.pdf

(Dietz) Story of his childhood – Richard B. Fry, *The Crimson and the Gray, 100 years with the WSU Cougars,* (Pullman, WA, Washington State University Press, 1989) p. 68

Dietz father's captivity: *Reader's Digest*, January 23, 1912, p. 160-161 (reprinted from *The New York Sun*

Sunday Night

Team practiced all day: Girard Clark, Interview with Girard Clark, son of football Captain Asa Clark, by author Pullman WA October 18, 1997

Dietz comes down with pneumonia fear: *Evergreen*, October 7, 1915 p. 3

Night Practice

Oregon preview: *Evergreen*, October 7 1915, front page

Dietz showed film: Girard Clark, Interview with Girard Clark, son of football Captain Asa Clark, by author Pullman WA October 18, 1997

Dietz uses film: *Seattle Star*, November 6, 1915 p. 7

Chapter 2: Oregon

Oregon

Reason to be confident: *Pullman Herald*, October 8, 1915 front page

"I can't hear you boys" Bezdek: *Evergreen*, October 13, 1915, p. 5

Rally

No women at rally: *Evergreen* October 13, 1915 p. 5

"fairly even" Clark: *Evergreen* October 8, 1915 front page

Kick-Off

Game summary: *Evergreen* October 20, 1915, p. 2 and *Pullman Herald*, October 15, 1915 front page, p. 6

"Hey Clark, you OK" Bohler: Girard Clark, Interview with Girard Clark, son of football Captain Asa Clark, by author Pullman WA October 18, 1997

Slugging and roughing it: *Evergreen* October 13, 1915, p. 3

Famous body blocking: *Evergreen* October 13, 1915, p. 3

Correspondents cheered – referee warning : *Evergreen* October 13, 1915, p. 3

"farmboys": Girard Clark, Interview with Girard Clark, son of football Captain Asa Clark, by author Pullman WA October 18, 1997

Chapter 3: Oregon Agricultural College

Oregon Agricultural College

Dietz to lead Art class: *Evergreen*, October 10, 1915 p. 6

Classwork

McCully offers peace prize: *Evergreen*, October 7, 1918 p. 9

Injuries: *Evergreen* October 13, 1915, front page

Everett May "Didn't make sense": *Evergreen* October 13, 1915 p. 2

William Nessly, H McB Hart to send dispatches: *Pullman Herald*, October 10, 1915 front page

Pug Barnes: *Evergreen*, October 20, 1915 front page

Heckler: *Evergreen*, October 20, 1915 p. 5

Game Summary: *Evergreen*, October 20, 1915 front page, p. 2

Dispatches to the dance: *Evergreen*, October 20, 1915 front page

Returning Victors

Injuries: *Pullman Herald*, October 22, 1915, p. 3

Dance proclamation: *Chinook 1917*, (Gateway Printing Co, Seattle WA, 1917) p. 358

Hack Applequist returns: *Chinook 1917*, (Gateway Printing Co, Seattle WA, 1917) p. 377

Pi Beta Phi: *Chinook 1917*, (Gateway Printing Co, Seattle WA, 1917) p. 377

Reaction

Wild night at Pullman: *Evergreen*, October 27, 1915 p. 2

Pasadena

We'd better go back to football: Joe Hendrickson, Tournament of Roses; the first 100 years, (Knapp Press, Los Angeles, CA 1989) p22

Dance of Champions

Clark and Bangs: *Chinook 1917*, (Gateway Printing Co, Seattle WA, 1917) p. 374-375

Varsity Ball: *Chinook 1917*, p. 206

Chapter 4: Idaho

Idaho

Winning streak: *Evergreen*, October 29, 1915 Special Edition, front page

Gambling: *Evergreen*, October 29, 1915 Special Edition, p. 4

Women will hike to game in Moscow: *Evergreen*, October 20 1915 front cover

Kick-off

Game Summary: *Evergreen*, November 3, 1915, front page

Bangs: PowWow and Interview with Girard Clark, son of football Captain Asa Clark, by author Pullman WA October 18, 1997

A New Voice

Roscoe: *Oregonian*, October 31, 1915; also *Evergreen*, November 3, 1915 front page

Pullman

"Football captain and his lady...had slats concealed beneath" *Chinook 1917*, p. 384 (Slats Olson is referenced only in the *Pullman Herald* and is not listed as a student)

Chapter 5: Montana

Montana

Game preps: *Evergreen*, November 3, 1915 front page

Rose Bowl Selection

Rube Samuelsen, *The Rose Bowl Game*, (Garden City, N.Y. Doubleday and Co,1951) p. 12

Casey Shearer, *The Road to Pasadena*, Brown University Alumni Magazine, September 2000 p. 6

Infirmary

"Many profs on the sick list… "old Crow," *Chinook 1917*, October 30 p. 358

Game

Game Summary: *Evergreen*, November 10, 1915, front page

Washington

California had just added football this first season: *Evergreen*, September 30, 1915 p. 11

Dobie unhappy, Fans threw peanuts" "Legendary coach Gil Dobie's only loss at Washington: his legacy" *Seattle Times*, November 20, 2010

Dinner/Recovery

Evergreen, November 10, 1915 p. 4

Clark fell asleep: Interview with Girard Clark, son of football Captain Asa Clark, by author Pullman WA October 18, 1997

Chapter 6: Whitman

Whitman

Red skinned aborigine: *Spokane Daily Chronicle*, November 8 1915, p. 12

Dietz casually walks sideline: *Spokane Daily Chronicle*, November 8 1915, p. 12

Markers on road: *Evergreen*, November 10, 1915 front page

Leather Gloves

Gloves: *Evergreen*, November 17, 1915 p. 2

Fans

Clark letter to editor for fans: *Evergreen*, November 10 1915 p. 5

Telegram to Bender: *Evergreen,* October 20, 1915 p. 5

Kick-Off

Game summary: *Evergreen,* November 17, 1915

Dietz Interview: "Seattle Star," *Evergreen,* November 17, 1915

Rose Bowl

California had just added football this first season: *Evergreen*, September 30, 1915 p. 11

Rube Samuelsen, *The Rose Bowl Game,* (Garden City, N.Y. Doubleday and Co,1951) p. 12

Casey Shearer, *The Road to Pasadena,* Brown University Alumni Magazine, September 2000 p. 6

Benjay: Keep a Goin', p. 120

Dobie – Not playing WSC, Fewer UW students, not happy: *Evergreen*, November 24, 1915, p. 2

Newspapers hailed WSC champs: *Evergreen,* November 24, 1915 p. 2

New York Critic hails WSC: *Spokesman Chronicle,* November 13, 1915 p. 12

WSC wins championship: *Evergreen,* November 17, 1915 front page

Sportswriters laud WSC: *Evergreen,* November 17, 1915 p. 2

Trains to Gonzaga

Special train planned: *Evergreen,* November 24, 1915 front page

Newspapers hailed WSC champs: *Evergreen,* November 24, 1915 p. 2

Invitation

Kienholz telegram: *Pullman Herald,* November 19, 1915 front page

Awards

Gray W Awards: *Evergreen,* November 17, 1915 p. 2

Clark convinces Bohler: Interview with Girard Clark, son of football Captain Asa Clark, by author Pullman WA October 18, 1997

Acceptance

WSU Accepts: *Evergreen,* November 17, 1915 front page

California

California letter to Dietz; *Evergreen,* November 24, 1915, front page

Reaction – *Evergreen,* November 24, 1915, front page

Dietz meets with Cal in Spokane: *Spokane Daily Chronicle,* November 15, 1915 p. 14

Gray W

Gray W Awards: *Evergreen,* November 17, 1915 p. 2

Also: *Evergreen*, December 15, 1915 front page

Chapter 7: Gonzaga

Pullman

Champs of NW: *Evergreen*, November 24, 1915 p. 2, and *Pullman Herald* November 26, 1915 front page

Newspapers hailed WSC champs: *Evergreen*, November 24, 1915 p. 2

Contracts signed: *Evergreen*, November 17, 1915 front page

Booster train: *Evergreen*, November 24, 1915 front page

WSC getting great publicity: *Pullman Herald*, November 19, 1915 p. 3

Alumni to save Dietz: *Pullman Herald*, November 24, 1915 front page

Resignation

Dobie resigns: *Spokane Daily Chronicle*, November 22, 1915 p. 6

New Direction

Dietz and Bohler see UW play: *Seattle Star*, November 18, 1915 p. 7

Dietz not satisfied: *Spokane Daily Chronicle*, November 23, 1915 p. 17

Doane and Hanley out: *Evergreen*, November 24, 1915 p. 3

All League

Selections made: *Evergreen*, December 15, 1915 p. 2

Spokane Daily Chronicle, November 27, 1915 p. 12

Bangs for All-American: *Evergreen*, November 24, 1915, front page

Brown

Brown Selected*: Evergreen*, November 17, 1915 front page

Fans

400 tickets: *Spokane Daily Chronicle*, November 23, 1915, p. 6

Pub Barnes on train: *Spokane Daily Chronicle,* November 23, 1915, p. 6

Fans serpentine Spokane: *Spokane Daily Chronicle,* November 23, 1915, p. 6

Call to learn WSC songs: *Evergreen,* November 17, 1915 p. 5

Kick-Off

Game summary: *Evergreen*, December 1, 1915 front page

Dietz ran onto the field in protest at half: *Spokane Daily Chronicle,* November 24, 1915 p. 6

Pullman

Lillian McDonald: *Chinook 1917*, p. 64

Logistics

Bohler: Letters between Bohler and Tournament of Roses, Bohler papers, Manuscripts and Archive Special Collections, Holland Library, Washington State University

Limited number of players: Interview with Girard Clark, son of football Captain Asa Clark, by author Pullman WA October 18, 1997

Kruegel: John Frederick Bohler Papers 1907-1956, Manuscripts, Archives, and Special Collections, Washington State University Libraries

Evergreen, December 15, 1915 p. 2

Hollywood Calling

Dietz depiction of Indians: Tom Benjay, *Keep A Goin'* (Tuxedo Press, Carlisle PA 2006) p. 148 also William Dietz, "How Art Misrepresents the Indian" (*The Literary Digest* January 1912)

featured in "How Art Misrepresents the Indian."

Selig Benjay p. 131

Paid $100: Benjay p. 131

Brown

Playbook and Signals: *Pullman Herald*, December 10, 1915 p. 8

Brown beats Carlisle: *Evergreen*, December 15

Brown smothers Carlisle 39-3: *Spokane Daily Chronicle*, November 24, 1915 p. 6

Pullman Preps

Fans gathered Thorpe's Smokehouse on Main Street: *Crimson*, p. 81

Blankets

Tom Benjay, *Keep A Goin'* (Tuxedo Press, Carlisle PA 2006) p. 308

Chapter 8: Rose Bowl

Pullman Departure

Wheat prices: USDA http://www.automationinformation.com/Favorites/wheat_prices.htm

Montana: Tom Benjey, *Keep a' Goin'* p. 121

Montana: Richard B. Fry, *The Crimson and the Gray, 100 years with the WSU Cougars,* (Pullman, WA, Washington State University Press, 1989) p. 79

Dietz prepares Indian songs: *Evergreen*, November 24, 1915, p. 7

San Francisco

Itinerary: *Evergreen*, December 15, 1915 p. 3

Christmas Morning

Team arrives: *Pullman Herald,* December 31, 1915 front page

California

Schedule: *Pullman Herald,* December 3, 1915 p. 2

Bertonneau: Rube Samuelsen, *The Rose Bowl Game*, (Garden City, N.Y. Doubleday and Co, 1951) p. 12

Distances

Lillian and Helen friends, would meet: Interview with Girard Clark, son of football Captain Asa Clark, by author Pullman WA October 18, 1997

Pasadena

Party, racing: *PowWow*, February 16, 1916 p. 13 and *Evergreen*, January 15, 1916 p. 8

Spokane

Newspaper reports: *PowWow*, February 16, 1916 p. 13

Encounters

Studio: Interview with Girard Clark, son of football Captain Asa Clark, by author Pullman WA October 18, 1997. Also *PowWow*, February 16, 1916 p. 13

Spokane

Newspaper reports: *PowWow*, February 16, 1916 p. 13

Practice

Cancelled practice: Clark interview, 1983, cited in *Crimson and Grey* by Dick Frye, p. 72; also in *PowWow*, February 16, 1916 p. 13

Movie Making

Dick Hanley letter: Maxwell Stiles, *The Rose Bowl*, (Nash-U-Nal Publications/Sportsmaster Publications, Los Angeles, CA 1945) p. 11

Also: Rube Samuelsen, *The Rose Bowl Game*, (Garden City, N.Y. Doubleday and Co, 1951) p. 12

Strategy

Dietz visit: Interview with Girard Clark, son of football Captain Asa Clark, by author Pullman WA October 18, 1997

A Wrap

Football scene: Interview with Girard Clark, son of football Captain Asa Clark, by author Pullman WA October 18, 1997. Also, Benjey, *Keep A Goin'* p. 131-132, and Hanley letter: Maxwell Stiles, *The Rose Bowl*, (Nash-U-Nal Publications/Sportsmaster Publications, Los Angeles, CA 1945) p. 11

Tournament of Roses Parade

Dietz troubled: Interview with Girard Clark, son of football Captain Asa Clark, by author Pullman WA October 18, 1997

Trouble

Massive ball New Year's Eve: *Pullman Herald,* December 31, 1915 front page

(Dietz) …predicted a defeat for his charges" "…especially worried about Pollard" *Spokane Daily Chronicle* December 31, 1915 p. 6

Premonition: Tom Benjey, *Keep A Goin', The Life of Lone Star Dietz,* (Carlisle, PA Tuxedo Press, 2006) p. 100

Revelations

Bohler conversation: Carl Dietz: Interview with Girard Clark, son of football Captain Asa Clark, by author Pullman WA October 18, 1997

Pullman

Fans gathered Thorpe's Smokehouse on Main Street: *Crimson,* p. 81

Thorpe's Smokehouse: *Pullman Herald,* December 31, 1915 front page

Photo of football field on wall: Manuscripts, Archives, and Special Collections, Washington State University Libraries

Frenzy of excitement: *Pullman Herald*, January 7, 1916 p. 3

The Rose Bowl

Game summary: *Evergreen*, January 15, 1916 p. 2

Also: *Los Angeles Examiner*, January 1916 via *Pullman Herald*, January 7 1916 front page

Premonitions

Carl Dietz: Interview with Girard Clark, son of football Captain Asa Clark, by author Pullman WA October 18, 1997

Game Time

Game summary: *Evergreen*, January 15, 1916 p. 2

Also: *Los Angeles Examiner*, January 1916 via *Pullman Herald*, January 7, 1916 front page

Tickets: Tom Benjey, *Keep A' Goin'* p. 137-39

Warmups

Team warmed up in rain: *Crimson and Grey*, p. 81

Field conditions: Tom Benjey, *Keep A' Goin'* p. 137-39

Warmups: Frye, *Crimson and Grey*, p. 81

Kick-Off

Game summary: *Evergreen*, January 15, 1916 p. 2

Huge crowds: WSC Alumni Magazine *Pow Wow*, February 1916 p. 2-4

Also: *Los Angeles Examiner*, January 1916 via *Pullman Herald*, January 7 1916 front page

Pullman

Telegrams located in City of Pullman Image Collection, 1916 WSU Libraries MASC

Halftime

Game Summary: *Pullman Herald*, January 7, 1916 front page

Dietz: Interview with Girard Clark, son of football Captain Asa Clark, by author Pullman WA October 18, 1997

Brown

Brown react: Casey Shearer, *Brown Alumni Magazine*, September, 2000

Second Half

Game Summary: *Pullman Herald*, January 7, 1916 front page

Pullman

Reaction: Tom Benjey, *Keep A' Goin'* p. 141-142

Pasadena

Newspaper account: WSC Alumni Magazine *Pow Wow*, February 1916 p. 2-4

Dance of Champions

Betting - Dick Hanley letter: Maxwell Stiles, *The Rose Bowl*, (Nash-

U-Nal Publications/Sportsmaster Publications, Los Angeles, CA 1945) p. 11

Also: Rube Samuelsen, *The Rose Bowl Game*, (Garden City, NY, Doubleday and Co, 1951) p. 12

Champions Return

Dance summary: *Evergreen*, January 12, 1916 front page

Telegrams: WSC Alumni Magazine *PowWow*, February 1916 p. 2-4

Trains

Trip of warriors: WSC Alumni magazine *PowWow*, February 1916 p. 13

Players surprised: Interview with Girard Clark, son of football Captain Asa Clark, by author Pullman WA, October 18, 1997

Pullman

Players return: *Pullman Herald*, January 7 1916, front page

Best part being home: WSC Alumni magazine *PowWow*, February 1916 p. 13

Chapter 9: Endings

Duplicity Ends

Lister meeting: What really happened in 1917 for med Schools: *Spokesman Review*, March 14, 2015

Dobie: Daves, Porter and Porter: *The Glory of Washington: The People and Events That Shaped the Husky Athletic Tradition*, (Sports

Publishing Inc., Seattle WA, 2001) p. 64

Dietz: John Hibner, *Lone Star Dietz*, College Football Historical Society, Volume one, Number 5, August 1988 and Tom Benjey, *Keep A Goin'* p. 81

Carlisle connection: Dietz – 1915-1918, Gus Welch 1919-1922, Albert Exendine 1923-25

Reunion: Jimmy Jemail, *Sports Illustrated*, January 21, 1956

Disillusioned Tournament Group: Rube Samuelsen, *The Rose Bowl Game*, (Garden City, N.Y. Doubleday and Co,1951) p. 15

Love and Marriage

"Benton Bangs...loses his frat pin": *Chinook 1917*, (Gateway Printing Co, Seattle WA, 1917) p. 360

"Senior memorial bench where football captain lost his Frat Pin" *Chinook 1917*, (Gateway Printing Co, Seattle WA, 1917) p. 391

Clark

Clark: WSC Alumni magazine *Powwow*, 1935, October p. 4 and Jimmy Jemail, *Sports Illustrated*, January 21, 1956 n.p.

Bangs

Bangs: WSC Alumni magazine *Powwow*, 1935, October p. 4 and Jimmy Jemail, *Sports Illustrated*, January 21, 1956 n.p.

Bryan

Bryan: Enoch Bryan, *Historical Sketch of the State College of Washington 1890-1925*, (Spokane, WA Inland American Printing, 1925)

Bohler

Bohler: WSU Libraries, Manuscripts Archives and Special Collections

http://ntserver1.wsulibs.wsu.edu/masc/finders/cg502.htm

Durham

Durham: WSC Alumni magazine *Powwow*, 1935, October p. 4 and Jimmy Jemail, *Sports Illustrated*, January 21, 1956 n.p.

Zimmerman

Zimmerman: WSC Alumni magazine *Powwow*, 1935, October p. 4 and Jimmy Jemail, *Sports Illustrated*, January 21, 1956 n.p.

D. Hanley

D Hanley: WSC Alumni magazine *Powwow*, 1935, October p. 4

L. Hanley

L Hanley: WSC Alumni magazine *Powwow*, 1935, October p. 4 and Jimmy Jemail, *Sports Illustrated*, January 21, 1956 n.p.

Langdon

Langdon: WSC Alumni magazine *Powwow*, 1935, October p. 4

Applequist

Applequist: WSC Alumni magazine *Powwow*, 1935, October p. 4

WSU athletics website

Fishback

Fishback: WSU Alumni magazine Powwow, 1929, p. 11, and Powwow February, 1918 p. 10

Carl Dietz

Carl Dietz: WSC Alumni magazine *Powwow,* 1935, October p. 4

Pollard

http://fritzpollard.org/in-memoriam/fritz-pollard/

Kruegel

Kruegel: History of WSU buildings wsulibs.wsu.edu

A Century Back, WSU History wsm.wsu.edu

Wade

http://library.duke.edu/rubenstein/uarchives/history/articles/wade

Epilogue

Dietz epitaph: John C. Ewers, *Montana: The Magazine of Western History*, Volume XXVII, Number One, Winter 1977, p. 12

Hibner, *College Football Historical Society,* Vol 1, No. 5 August 1988